IN THE EYE OF THE
STORM

Walter E. Massey

IN THE EYE OF THE
STORM

My Time As Chairman of Bank of America During the Country's Worst Financial Crisis

Walter E. Massey

WITH ROSALIND KILKENNY MCLYMONT

Foreword by Dr. Ruth J. Simmons
President, Prairie View A&M University

Beckham
Publications

Silver Spring

Published in the United States by
Beckham Publications Co.
Silver Spring, MD 20904
ISBN: 978-0-931761-99-7

LCCN 2020908104

This book is dedicated to my late mother, Essie Nelson Massey, who set me on the right path in life, and to my wife, Shirley Anne Massey, who has kept me on that path, mostly, for over fifty years.

CONTENTS

ACKNOWLEDGMENTS

Writing this memoir has truly been a group effort in many ways. It is my story, but the telling of it is the result of a lot of input and assistance from many friends and colleagues.

Colin Campbell, a longtime friend and former newspaper columnist, strongly urged me to begin writing shortly after my encounter with the stranger at the Woods Hole Golf Club. Colin eventually helped me to write a first version of my life story, from which this memoir is extracted. Adrienne Harris, my chief of staff and speechwriter at Morehouse and a very close friend, critiqued, edited and rewrote much of the earlier material. Her knowledge of my 'voice' was very helpful. Mara Naselli, a professional writer and teacher, gave me great advice and feedback, especially on doing research about Hattiesburg, from which I learned things that I was not aware of when I started writing this memoir.

My old friend Avon Kirkland read several versions and excerpts and, based on his experience as a writer and TV producer, provided excellent and often tough feedback. Julie Taylor, our oldest Cape Cod friend; Chad Gifford, my partner in all of the bank adventures; and my other colleagues on the Special Committee have my sincere thanks for reading excerpts and providing encouragement throughout my writing this material.

My neighbor and good friend, Marianne 'Gini' Hartzmark, a widely published mystery writer, not only gave me great advice on story telling and scene setting, but also cooked wonderful meals for me when I came home after my colon operation in 2008.

Kerry Stapley, my developmental editor, provided essential advice on structure and phrasing that greatly improved earlier versions of this work. A special thanks goes to my good friend and colleague, Ruth Simmons, for taking the time to write such a generous and eloquent Foreword that really sets the theme for the memoir.

The bulk of my appreciation goes to Rosalind Kilkenny McLymont, who was a joy to work with and the key to getting this work completed. And without the encouragement, urging, pushing and constant support of my publisher and old friend, Barry Beckham, this would not have happened at all.

Finally, my grandchildren Eva and Artem have been and continue to be a constant source of inspiration. And, of course, the life I have led would not have been possible without the love and support of my lifelong partner, Shirley, to whom this work is dedicated.

INTRODUCTION

I could have called this book "A Life of Serendipity" because that theme rears its head throughout.

A serendipitous encounter was the initial impetus, which led me to contemplate writing my memoirs. I was in Cape Cod, my summer home, watching my grandchildren's tennis lessons when a woman whose grandchildren were also hard at work on their tennis game, sat down beside me and struck up a conversation. We were at the Woods Hole Golf Club, an upscale members-only club with arresting views of the Cape and beautiful, traditional clay tennis courts nestled in the trees on a bluff overlooking Buzzards Bay. I was a member and played tennis there regularly.

I did not recognize the woman. She told me she was not from the area but was visiting her daughter for the summer. She was an open, outgoing person who was clearly enjoying the setting and the opportunity to talk. We exchanged pleasantries, talking about our lives and families, our grandchildren, and the people we knew. It turned out we knew a few people in common. She asked me a lot of questions and seemed fascinated by my various experiences. It was easy to chat with her.

When I was about to leave, she suddenly turned to me and said, "You know, you should write your story." She went on to say it was important for people to read my story. They would love it, she said, and, if nothing else, I owed it to my grandchildren.

I had never met this lady before, but she spoke with such intensity and directness that I began to think seriously about writing my memoir. That's when the idea for this effort was launched.

Sometimes I think my life looks like a canvas painted by Romare Bearden. The main subject sits in the center on a couch as planned, and then suddenly, bumping wildly into the composition is a framed drawing on the wall and a dog on the floor, and they seem like perfectly natural installments. And while I never expected to see any significance between the drawing on the wall and the dog on the floor, the connection was there all along. Like many of Bearden's paintings, life is never composed in a straight line. Certainly, mine hasn't been.

So, I left that inspiring conversation on a bench at the Woods Hole Golf Club, resolved to begin writing my memoir. That day, in the sun by the tennis court, unexpectedly meeting a friendly stranger, was the tipping point.

"You should write your story," she said.

I didn't mention the encounter to my wife, Shirley, or to the kids, but I knew I had to do this. My subconscious voice kept assailing me with questions, and I had answers for all of them. I always liked solving physics problems in solitude, so I was comfortable sitting alone, contemplating the project.

Generally speaking, I'm an unassuming person. But I do realize that I have achieved quite a bit. Although my accomplishments have largely been the result of my abilities and hard work, I know that support from others, along with timing, have been major and indispensable contributors to my successes.

So, why should I follow that stranger's suggestion? What could be the value of my story?

Her reasoning made sense. My story could further motivate those who are already on track to advance in their careers. Others who lack self-confidence could be stimulated to aim for the next level. I think of the person I used to be: the diffident sixteen-year-old black boy leaving Hattiesburg, Mississippi, to enter the intimidating world of Morehouse College in Atlanta,

Georgia. How different would he have been if he had known it would all turn out like this?

And what about my grandchildren? The woman declared that I owed the book of my life to them as a measure of my love for them, and as patriarchal instruction for them. Who else might be interested? Maybe many others who have never heard of me ... until the memoir is announced and published.

Later that afternoon, alone in a chair, I replayed the moments that were essential to my growth and development. My times at Morehouse College, Brown University, the University of Chicago, the Argonne National Laboratory, and the National Science Foundation — all the ways those places connected me with the wonderful world of theoretical physics would be instrumental. And who has been more instrumental in guiding and supporting me than my wife of fifty years, Shirley Anne Massey, who, at that moment, was upstairs with our grandkids.

Like eliminating some unknowns in a scientific experiment, my review led me to see that there were too many stories to fit into one book. I would do better breaking down my wide range of experiences into several memoirs. I needed a more focused approach where I could describe one of the single periods in my life that has been most consequential.

This past September, the anniversary of the 2008/2009 financial crisis, led me to re-examine that period in my life. Since I was so critically engaged in that drama, I felt I must write about it, and I had to do it now. I don't think anyone else can write about those times from the unique perspective I had as Chairman of Bank of America.

I hope readers, my grandchildren included, will learn or recall, something about that very scary period. Equally importantly, I hope they will appreciate how one individual – in this case, me — managed a crisis in a leadership role that was neither sought, nor expected, but rather, was thrust upon him. I hope they will take away some lessons to apply to their own lives.

So here it is — my first memoir.

FOREWORD

Anyone even remotely aware of the extraordinary expanse of Walter Massey's educational, civic, and corporate contributions over the past five decades will be grateful to the stranger he evokes in the introduction to Volume One of his memoirs.

As he relates an encounter with a woman who, hearing about his life, encourages him to tell his story, one wonders why it took this chance meeting with a stranger to enlighten Massey about the importance of recording his invaluable insights from astoundingly varied leadership experiences.

To learn what motivated him in his youth to leave Hattiesburg, Mississippi, to studying physics at Morehouse College is to begin to understand how he persevered and excelled as one of a small number of African Americans in theoretical physics. Further, to understand what enabled him to overcome the significant barriers that existed for African American academics when he began his career, and to learn how he mediated the obstacles that would have so easily blocked the path of others, is to unlock the puzzle of why he managed to do what would have taken others more than two lifetimes to accomplish.

In recording for posterity, the twists and turns of his life and career, Dr. Massey begins closer to the end of his journey than to the beginning. By starting with how he became Chairman of the Board of Directors of Bank of America during the banking crisis of 2008, he chose to tackle what some would have thought might be the most difficult episode to write about. Taking over as Chairman at a perilous time, when not only shareholders, but also regulators, were demanding significant change at the bank, he might well have found it especially difficult and sensitive to relate what was happening behind the scenes as internal politics was leading to difficult conversations, government officials were issuing dire warnings, public anger and protests were erupting, and the path to board consensus on a course of action was far from clear. Yet, Massey gives us access to this world with clarity, candor, and affability that will no doubt surprise many.

Therein lies the greatest value of this story, as told by an academic of Massey's stature and experience. While some always find it odd to see members of the academy straddle sectors, Massey reveals that it was the nature of his academic training that enabled him to deal with business environments that appear antithetical to the university environment. In the case of his directorships of public companies (British Petroleum, McDonald's, Motorola and others), it was precisely the knowledge and skills acquired in pursuing a Ph.D., serving as a professor, and subsequently, as an administrator that gave him insights that enabled him to be a leader in the corporate sector. Such qualities and skills as knowledge of human psychology, an empathetic stance toward others, an understanding of the benefits of rigorous thought, a commitment to building consensus, and the willingness and self-confidence to lead fit just as well in banking as in academic leadership.

Rigorous thought and intellectual honesty require the telling of his Bank of America chairmanship as more than a mere series of actions. For one as committed to the academic life as Massey has been, it would be difficult to open the door only slightly to what transpired. Committed to truth-telling, he knew that opening wide the access to how this history had unfolded would be essential. Along the way, he not only discloses what few would have felt able to disclose of the inner workings of bank leadership, but he also helps us to understand why he is empowered to tell the story in this way. Hauntingly, at every turn, the image of his younger self growing up in segregated Mississippi is the constant counterpoint to the heights of power being depicted. The wonderment of that young boy at how far his older-self managed to travel, in spite of the trenchant racism that shaped his early life, is the compelling leitmotif of the narrative.

People may have the luxury today of forgetting how brutal the racial divide was during the time of Massey's youth and coming of age. Massey recalls it vividly as a helpful backdrop for his unending surprise at every milestone that he scaled. First, as a faculty member at the University of Illinois, then, as a scientist at Argonne National Laboratory, a Dean at Brown, Director of the National Science Foundation, Director of Argonne National Laboratory, Provost of the University of California System, and President of Morehouse College, he excelled wherever he went. At each turn, he reacts in genuine awe at the distance he has traveled from segregated Hattiesburg, Mississippi. But even as he marvels at the opportunities he has had, one senses that he may still be missing the bigger picture: that no matter one's origins, to accomplish just a fraction of these achievements would be remarkable; to accomplish so many is no longer a story of mere wonder. It is the stuff of legends.

While relating these experiences, Massey pauses from time-to-time to reveal trusted friendships, mentorships that made a difference in his career, failures that caused him to stumble momentarily, the triumphant marriage to his wife, Shirley, that empowered so many of his accomplishments, and the satisfaction of fatherhood. Without dwelling on these details in this memoir, he introduces these important elements of his personal life as a means of helping us understand how he became *the* Walter Massey.

What powered the energy, patience, and determination of this man across so many decades? He promises that the full extent of the primary influences in his life will be told in later volumes. One hopes that those volumes come soon, as the story of his life is one that is important for young scholars and other achievers who face the future with trepidation. Recently, minority youth have begun to worry about what they often perceive to be the overwhelming odds against their succeeding in the way they and their parents wish. Walter Massey's story reveals what is possible through education and determination, even when resources are constrained, hope is limited, and barriers seem impenetrable.

Ruth J. Simmons, Ph.D.
Prairie View, Texas

CHAPTER ONE

"WALTER, DO YOU HAVE TIME TO DO THIS JOB?"

On the morning of April 29, 2009, I awoke much earlier than usual. It was the day of Bank of America's annual shareholders' meeting in Charlotte, North Carolina. As a member of the Board of Directors, I was in town for it. But before this meeting, I had to attend another, the meeting of the board's Audit Committee. That began at seven, a good three hours before the shareholders' meeting was scheduled to start. When I was actively doing theoretical physics research, I worked very late at night, long after Shirley and the kids went to bed, and slept late in the mornings, until about nine o'clock. I still don't like getting up before eight o'clock or so.

I usually jumpstart the day with a very hot shower, which I did that morning. Fortunately, breakfast would be served at the meeting, so that gave me a little extra time to linger in my hotel room. I turned on the TV to get the local weather and opened the curtains to let in the sunlight. It seemed to be a decent day. At home in Chicago, first thing in the morning, my wife Shirley and I usually turned on the local news or the weather channel, Shirley's favorite. I gave Shirley a call even though it was an hour earlier in Chicago. I knew she would be awake, expecting to hear from me.

1

"I called you last night after the board dinner, and you didn't answer," I said when she picked up the phone.

"You know I always go to bed early when you aren't here," she replied.

"Yes, I know. But don't you think eight-thirty is a bit too early even for you?" I joked.

"Well, I went to sleep. How are you? Are you nervous?"

"No. But I am anxious. It's going to be a contentious annual meeting, I'm sure."

"Too bad it won't be on TV. Be sure to call me when it's over."

"Ok. I have to go now. Love you."

"And I, you," she said warmly.

I hung up and scanned the headlines in the newspapers that had been slipped under the door of my room, glancing at the TV every now and then. I was certain there would be news about the shareholders' meeting. There was — in the newspapers and on TV.

I left my room at about 6:45 and headed to the Audit Committee meeting at the bank's headquarters. It was a quick walk because there is direct access from the hotel to the headquarters building next door.

So began one of the most fateful days in my life.

I had joined the old San Francisco-based BankAmerica board in 1993 before we merged with NationsBank Corporation and became Bank of America. This year's shareholder meeting wouldn't be like those of past years. The board was currently under a lot of pressure. We had just purchased Merrill Lynch, the venerable investment bank, for fifty-billion-dollars, and this brought criticism from our shareholders, the media, and the greater financial community. Though we had completed the purchase in December, it wasn't until the end of January that we'd announced the financial results of the acquisition. Everyone knew Merrill had been losing money. No one suspected it had lost so many billions of dollars until our fourth-quarter announcement, which made the figure public.

At that point, threats started rolling in. Shareholders complained vociferously, accusing the board and management of deliberately withholding material and reportable information from them before they voted to approve the merger and blaming the board for failing to assert the Material Adverse Clause, or MAC, in the purchase agreement that would have canceled the deal. Some people wanted certain committee chairs fired. Others wanted all eighteen members of the board replaced, and while that rarely happens in corporate America, these were not normal times. We were entering new territory in so many ways. I knew it was going to be a difficult meeting.

Shareholders vote on directors by name, individually, in board elections. Some of the bank's large shareholders had said they targeted specifically the chairs of important committees — the Compensation Committee in particular, and the Asset Quality Committee, which looks at the debt the company takes on, and the quality of its credit relationships. So, it was quite likely that some of us might be voted off the board.

Before I left Chicago, I said to Shirley, "Watch the headlines because you may find out that we've all been voted off the board. There could be another board without me on it."

Shirley had been putting away dishes from the dishwasher, but upon hearing this, she froze stock still in midstride. Her eyebrows flew up.

"Oh, really? Is it that serious?"

"Well, I think it could be. We're getting a lot of bad press. The shareholders are really upset."

I wasn't that upset about possibly having to leave the board. I was seventy-one, and at that time, board members at Bank of America had to retire at seventy-two. No matter what, I had only one more year on the board. Besides, our life in Chicago was already filled with all kinds of meaningful activities. We had moved back to Chicago in 2007 when I retired from my twelve-year stint as president of Morehouse College in Atlanta. I still served on the boards for McDonald's, the Mellon Foundation, and a few other organizations, and just recently had landed a dream assignment on the board for the United States Tennis Association, which meant seats in the president's suite for all US Open games. Shirley was heavily involved in community work, and both of us were thoroughly enjoying reconnecting with all of our old friends and getting re-engaged with Chicago.

However, I did think it would be highly embarrassing, and certainly damaging to my reputation to not be re-elected, especially considering I'd served on the board for almost sixteen years. Truthfully, though, my own position on the board was a minor concern compared to what was happening nationally in the financial markets. More than I worried about myself, I worried about the bank. The financial industry was still jittery after the collapse of some of its major players the previous fall. In September 2008, Washington Mutual, a savings and loan giant, had become the largest bank failure in U.S. history. Days later, Wachovia Corp., one of the largest retail banks in the country, was forced by federal regulators to merge with Wells Fargo. Rumors were rife that federal regulators were also deeply concerned about Citibank.

A great deal has been published about the infamously 'scary' weekend in 2008, from Friday, September 12, to Sunday, September 14, when it seemed as though the entire U.S. financial system might collapse. Mounting crises had precipitated a run on the banks to the tune of about a half-trillion dollars. The old, established Wall Street investment firm, Bear Stearns, had faltered and been absorbed by J.P. Morgan. Lehman Brothers were rumored to be next, and the financial media was saturated with stories reflecting serious concerns about Morgan Stanley.

As the number of crises spiked late in the year, Bank of America has often been deemed a 'white knight,' a savior of sorts, for one or another of Wall Street's troubled investment banks.

That is until we acquired Merrill Lynch.

Overnight we were saddled with $15.3 billion in losses that Merrill had piled up in its fourth quarter. Then, just before we took over on January 1, we learned Merrill paid its employees

$3.2 billion in bonuses. Normally, bonuses are paid at the end of January or in early February, but in anticipation of the restructuring, Merrill paid early. All of this came on top of our own losses in the fourth quarter. By the time the annual meeting came around, the bank's share price had dropped precipitously.

We were being sued for the way we handled disclosures about Merrill's financial health; we'd taken two government loans under the Troubled Asset Relief Program, commonly known as TARP, and we were under investigation by the New York attorney general, U.S. Congress, and bank regulators. The press touted the views of the larger financial community. They said we'd overpaid for Merrill Lynch, that we hadn't done due diligence leading up to the acquisition, and that we'd deceived our shareholders prior to their vote on the merger.

All of these claims are oversimplifications, and as such, are debatable. The idea that we'd overpaid is tough to prove; it always takes a while to know how deals like these will work out. It may be to the profit of all, just not right away. The second claim that we'd neglected our due diligence was based on the idea that Merrill Lynch was in much worse shape than it had outwardly seemed to be. The media pushed the narrative that greater inspections on our part may have revealed the rot at the bank's core before we acquired it. The third claim seemed to almost undermine the second. On the one hand, they were saying we hadn't done our research and didn't know how bad Merrill was. On the other hand, they were claiming that we knew full well the shape Merrill Lynch was in and hadn't been transparent with our shareholders. The whole situation was a mess, and the fact that the bank had legitimate responses to these allegations didn't spare us from criticism.

The worst thing any major corporation can do is to give the impression of instability at the top. Large shareholders want stability no matter how much they may disagree with management. But they'll send a message. For us, the message would come in the form of fewer affirmative votes to defend our membership on the board.

The bank's position weighed on my mind as I went into the shareholders' meeting. What were we going to do? What steps did we have to take to deal with the situation we were in?

In the days leading up to this meeting, even as I went about my normal daily routine at home, I asked myself these questions over and over, wracking my brain for answers I didn't have. Although these issues pressed hard on me, I agonized over what *I* could do to alleviate the situation.

"What is my role in all this? What can I, or should I, be doing now?"

I felt I had been a diligent board member, questioning management on their decisions, and giving my input. At this point, however, there was nothing to do but wait and see what the shareholders, who were the ultimate owners of the company, would decide.

Like most corporations in America, the bank had a combined chairman and chief executive officer. Kenneth "Ken" Lewis was the bank's CEO and its chairman of the board. He was a "star of American finance," according to *The New York Times*. *American Banker* named him 2008 Banker of the Year, citing his "vision" and his "daring conquests." But for the first time, there was a proposal on the shareholder proxy, the meeting's official agenda, to separate the chairman and chief executive roles from one another, and create a new position of non-executive chairman of the board. Shareholders were pushing for this because they thought the board needed to take a more assertive role in the oversight of the bank. They felt that as long as the chairman and CEO roles were combined, there would be too much power centralized in one person.

Overwhelmingly, the shareholders of large American corporations aren't individuals. Instead, they are other corporations, pension funds, or investment firms, and usually, these other companies can be trusted to vote in accordance with management on proxy issues. Our bank's management had recommended against splitting the two roles, but we thought the shareholders' proposal might carry the day. Large institutional investors like CalPERS, California's pension fund for public sector employees, had already cast their votes prior to the meeting, so we knew they supported the proposal. Furthermore, our own board secretary had warned us the proposal might pass. We knew where some of our large shareholders stood. Small shareholders still had to vote.

The night before the vote, I thought about who could fill Ken's shoes as chairman of the board if the position was split. I went through the names of the board members I could support. I knew the Executive Committee would be thinking about this, but we'd all have to vote.

The meeting was held, as usual, in the Belk Theater at the North Carolina Blumenthal Performing Arts Center in the heart of "Uptown Charlotte." Bank of America's corporate headquarters, a tower stretching sixty stories high, is located in the same complex as the Blumenthal. Directors stay at The Ritz-Carlton next door, which links to the complex by a walkway.

Someone from the bank's staff came and escorted each of us to the auditorium. We were led in through a back way so that we didn't see what was going on in the street. We assumed there were protesters. There always are. In the following day's *New York Times*, there was a picture of a woman in a T-shirt that read, "Fire!!! Kenneth Lewis. Fire!!! The Board of Directors. Clean Sweep." The words were printed in big, bold letters.

Usually, there aren't too many reporters who cover these meetings, but this was special. The shareholders' complaints had been in the news for weeks. The board didn't try to secret itself in any way. Yes, we went into the theater through a back corridor, but that is normal. When you're a director of a major corporation, you have to assume you may be a target to someone.

I was still making my final decision of who among the many distinguished members of the board — CEOs, a four-star general, and successful entrepreneurs — would get my vote for chairperson. Plus, I was hoping that the meeting wouldn't be too raucous. I'd been at rowdy shareholder meetings where people insulted the CEO and called for the board to be fired. I was on the board of British Petroleum from 1998 to 2008, and for those meetings, we had not only a driver but also a bodyguard. Organizations like Green Peace and more extreme environmental groups would frequently disrupt the meetings. I was anxious to get through this one without any major issue or drama unfolding. I just wanted to get to the boardroom and have the board meeting.

Typically, the day's running order would begin with committee meetings in the early morning, followed by a shareholder meeting around ten o'clock. After all that, there was a brief meeting of the board of directors to re-elect officers and re-establish committees. The auditorium was filled to capacity when we arrived. We deliberately got there just a few minutes before the meeting started. The theater seats twenty-one-hundred people. By the bank's count, twenty-two hundred showed up. They spilled over into the lobby to watch the proceedings on video monitors.

Inside the auditorium, the air crackled with excitement and tension. But cordiality and respect held their ground. The board wasn't roped off or segregated in any way, and quite a few shareholders approached us to say hello, especially to the directors who were from the local area and to those they knew personally. No one shouted at us. I didn't even catch anyone giving us the evil eye, though I wouldn't be surprised if some shareholders were.

Directors and senior bank officers sit together in the first and second rows of the auditorium. Ken, as chair of the meeting; Alice Herald, the corporate secretary, and official secretary for the meeting; and Joe Price, chief financial officer, sat on the stage.

I was sitting in the second row, next to Gary Countryman, the person I thought really would be good as chairman. I had a couple of others in mind, but Gary was a guy I really liked. He was a good board member: calm, very participative, collegial, and unpretentious. He was the chairman emeritus of the Liberty Mutual Group in Boston.

Gary always had a pleasant face. He carried himself as a low-key, engaging guy. There was nothing bombastic about him — nothing CEO-like. If you met him on the street, you would not guess he was a CEO. You'd sooner think he was a schoolteacher, so humble was his demeanor. In the board meetings, he didn't say a lot, but when he spoke, his remarks were always thoughtful. He came across as conversational, even when commenting on a very difficult subject. He was challenging but not aggressive.

As we waited for the meeting to begin, Gary leaned over to me and said, "Walter, I think this resolution to require a non-executive chairman is going to pass."

"So do I, Gary."

Then he said, "Walter, do you have time to do this job?"

I was speechless. I thought it was a joke. I wasn't a banker, and at that point, I had only one year to go before reaching the mandatory retirement age of 72.

"Are you kidding?" I said to Gary, "I'm thinking of you."

He said, "I'm serious, Walter. Some of us have talked about it, and we think you could do it. You'd be the person."

And then the meeting started, and we had to stop talking. I still believed that it was just Gary saying those things because he and I liked each other. I thought, "Yeah, Gary might be thinking that, but not the whole board."

CHAPTER TWO
WALTER E. MASSEY,
CHAIRMAN, BANK OF AMERICA

Without warning, the auditorium erupted in a roar of applause as Ken strode to the podium. His loyalists were on their feet. They whooped and cheered for more than half a minute, but didn't quite drown the boos of irate shareholders.

When the room quieted, Ken defended the Merrill Lynch acquisition. Backing out of the deal after the magnitude of Merrill's losses came to light could have dealt a deathblow to the country's battered financial system, and undermined confidence in the bank, he told them. Joe Price followed with a report on the bank's finances.

Then it was time for shareholders to ask questions. Microphones were set up in the aisles. Lines formed like ribbons behind them. Shareholders raised questions about the board's lack of deep banking experience. Questions turned into statements, most of which berated us for the situation we were in. Speakers singled out individual board members, especially those who chaired the committees on asset quality and compensation. Individuals who said they had lost thousands of dollars didn't repress their anger or bitterness. Some of the stories were quite sad and acted as a sobering reminder that at the end of every business decision are real people, whose lives may really be affected in many ways. Many who were against management spoke personally about Ken. They made accusations about his "lack of leadership;" how, as CEO and chairman, he'd "led the bank in the wrong direction. You and the board!"

One impressive gentleman from Texas, Jonathan Finger, excoriated Ken and the board. He ran an investment firm, Finger Interests, and owned just over a million Bank of America shares. His contention was we should not have gone through with the Merrill merger without another vote by the shareholders. He was very reasoned, but also implacable. He even led a television advertising campaign to rally shareholders behind his cause: ousting Ken as chairman.

However, quite a few people spoke positively about the bank and about Ken, like the representatives of Habitat for Humanity and several environmental groups. The bank had made a decision not to fund companies that were engaged in "mountaintop removal mining" for coal. Environmentalists had pushed for that decision and really lauded the bank for its stance.

Statements turned into speeches. Alice, the board secretary, would say to speakers, "You have two minutes to speak." Later, it would be, "You have thirty seconds left." Then, "Your time is up." Many ignored that. Ken, to his credit, did not cut them off.

I was very pleased with the way Ken was handling the meeting. He didn't get too ruffled as shareholders vented. He stood at the podium for most of the meeting, patient, stoic almost, except when he twiddled his thumbs and bit his lip.

Ken was a very good chairman and an adroit CEO. He and I were of different ages, races, and professions, but we had both come from small Southern towns and "made good." Born in Walnut Grove, Mississippi, about ninety miles from my native Hattiesburg, Mississippi, he grew up in small towns in Georgia and later attended Georgia State University in Atlanta. In my case, I wanted to get as far away from Hattiesburg's crushing racial environment as possible. While I did not suffer overt daily threats and insults, the fact remains there were dark and very dangerous aspects to life during my childhood. At any point, I, or any member of my family, could have been falsely accused or deliberately targeted for some offense of which we were not even aware. In looking back, it is as if we swam through shark-infested waters assuming that, if we did not disturb the sharks, they would not attack us; in retrospect, I've learned that this was an optimistic assumption at best, and probably even a dangerous one.

I've often thought that Ken had something to prove; that he could best the heads of other major banks even though he had not attended their prestigious colleges and universities. As Bank of America became more involved in investment banking, I think Ken's desire to out-compete those New York bankers grew even stronger.

Ken had a low-key sense of humor that would have surprised most people who didn't know him. He wasn't gregarious, a shake-and-bake kind of guy. Publicly and privately, he maintains a pretty steady temperament, pretty calm. I had great confidence in him. So did the board. We had voted unanimously to keep him on as Chairman and CEO, just as we unanimously supported the purchase of Merrill Lynch. I don't think we ever had a discussion wherein people said we shouldn't have bought it. Once we bought it, we just had to figure out how to deal with it.

If you've been to shareholder meetings as often as I have, you know what to expect from certain people. You always have people at the meeting who come just to vent. If you own one share, you're allowed to come and speak, so some people buy shares just to come and make statements. I don't get angry; it's par for the course. Frankly, in some sense, this time, we deserved the criticism. The board knew better than anyone what had taken place, so most of us understood the shareholders' concerns. Generally, that was the attitude of the directors. No one thought, "these people don't understand."

The meeting continued — heated and contentious, though not unruly.

CHAPTER TWO

Then, there was Evelyn Y. Davis.

Rarely was there much more excitement than the interruptions of this ubiquitous corporate gadfly, a shareholder in her seventies who owned stock in 120 companies. She brought turmoil to many company meetings. She sat five rows behind us, across the aisle on the left.

Evelyn Y. Davis published a newsletter called *Highlights and Lowlights of Annual Meetings*, which she used to berate companies. She called herself the "Queen of the Corporate Jungle." She wore colorful, outlandish outfits. At one infamous board meeting, not one of ours, she showed up in a bathing suit. She was a total misogynist, but she would insult not only women but also CEOs. But she liked and defended Ken. She'd flirt with him with statements like, "Well, Ken, you know you're one of my favorite people." And, "Ken, you're cute. You should get a better-looking corporate secretary. A beautiful woman like me."

Her antics, such as running up on the stage and kissing Ken on the cheek, lightened up the atmosphere, even for the serious attendees who were irritated by her taking up so much time. You couldn't sit Evelyn down. She jumped up and fired off questions when Ken and Joe Price were giving their reports, even though that was not the time for questions. She'd embarrass anybody. Ken was very patient with her.

Our shareholder meetings normally lasted an hour to an hour-and-a-half. This one lasted four hours. As the votes were being tallied, it became increasingly clear that the resolution to split the jobs of chairman and CEO would succeed. In the end, 50.34 percent of the shareholders voted in favor of the split. Others voted to remove Ken from the board altogether.

When we came out of the meeting, we all sighed to ourselves, "Well, that's over. And all things considered, it wasn't so bad."

It was time now for the board to meet.

To get to the boardroom, we would have to exit the Blumenthal building which opens up into an enclosed vaulted atrium, walk across the floor to the bank's corporate center, get

13

IN THE EYE OF THE STORM

on an elevator, and ride up to the 30th floor, where the elevator opened to a foyer that led to the boardroom itself. The foyer looks out over the Bank of America Stadium, headquarters of the National Football League team, the Carolina Panthers. A small sitting area near the window offers a very pleasant view, and when I'm there, I usually pause to take it in. Not this morning, though. The meeting was about to start, and I had to go to the men's room.

As I was walking toward the boardroom on my way from the restroom, I saw Ken waiting in the foyer. He pulled me aside. The other directors had already gone into the boardroom.

"Walter, you got a minute?"

"Of course," I said, thinking this a bit unusual. Ken always started meetings punctually.

We sat down on a little bench. I suspected he wanted to ask what I thought about so-and-so becoming chairman. But I was wrong.

Ken said, "Walter" — I don't remember his exact words, but it was either "the executive committee" or "the governance committee" — "met this morning, and we talked to the board, and we'd like for you to be our new chairman."

Right then, it just didn't register.

It's hard to describe the feeling. It's like something happening, and you can't even reflect on it because the very idea is too surreal.

"Oh shit!" I heard myself say.

It just popped out.

Ken just looked at me.

"Are you serious?" I asked, regaining composure.

"Yes."

"Ken," I said, "I don't think this makes any sense. I'm not a banker. We've just been accused of not having enough banking competence on the board. I don't think this is good for the bank."

His response was, "Well, we've thought about it, Walter. People on the board admire you. People think you have a great sense of integrity. You have contacts nationally. You're well

14

known. You've been on the board for almost sixteen years; you understand how the board operates, and all of the directors have the utmost confidence in you."

"Are you sure?" I was incredulous.

"Of course!" he responded. "We think you are the person."

To Ken, it was like, "This is so obvious, I don't see why you don't think it is obvious." That's how he presented his reasoning. That made me feel a little more confident. If he had been at all tentative, I would have felt otherwise. But he wasn't. He was just matter-of-fact.

I said, "Okay. You're sure?"

"We're sure."

I asked him how long I had to make up my mind.

Ken looked directly into my eyes and said, "About two minutes. Before we start the board meeting."

My nerves were jittery. "If you're serious about this, Ken, then okay."

So, we entered the boardroom. I looked for but saw no particular reaction from anyone. And the meeting began.

We went through the minutes and all the board news, and then we heard the report of the executive and governance committees. O. Temple Sloan, the lead director, gave the reports. And then he said, "As you know, the shareholders voted that we should have a separate chairman. We don't have to accept that."

We didn't. Shareholders' resolutions are mostly advisory. The board could ignore them, but you do that at your own peril because these are your shareholders, and they can sell the stock and go elsewhere. But you can disregard a resolution and sometimes you do when you feel it isn't the right vote.

Temple continued, "But we decided we should, and we're recommending that Walter Massey become chair."

Everyone turned to me and applauded. Nobody looked surprised. I still can't figure out how they all knew. Was it Ken? Or the Executive Committee? They couldn't have had a meeting of the board without me. So how did they all know? Or did they know? But they didn't seem surprised.

"Wait!" I said before anyone could call for a vote. "I really appreciate this. I'm honored, but I really want this to be serious. I think you really need to think about it without me." I didn't know if they already had. I didn't see how they could have met without me. It was just not logistically possible. They couldn't have called a secret meeting. Maybe they could have done it over the phone. I've never asked.

"I'm going to leave the room," I remember saying, "and I'd really like for you to make sure that this is what you want."

I left, somewhat dazed. As I was entering the foyer, J. Steele Alphin, the bank's chief administrative officer and Ken's chief of staff, was standing there.

Steele was a handsome gentleman with a rugged face and silvery-grey hair. He looked and sounded like he could be cast in a movie as a Virginia gentleman. He spoke with that soft Southern accent that some Virginians have. I always assumed he came from one of those old distinguished families that went back to Thomas Jefferson. I later learned that he came from fairly modest circumstances and had to work his way through college.

I always felt I could trust Steele. Not everyone liked him. He made tough decisions on behalf of Ken, maybe of his own volition, and those created controversy.

He approached me in the foyer. I said, "Are you behind this, Steele?" Because he was the real go-to person if you wanted to get to Ken.

He said, looking me straight in the eye. "No, Walter. The board is behind you. You need to do this. Ken needs you, and the bank needs you." He was deadly serious.

"Steele, I'm going to need all the help I can get."

"Don't worry, Walter. I have your back."

A few minutes later, Alice came out and escorted me back inside. The board greeted me with a standing ovation. What a moment! It was euphoric. All I could think was, "Wait till Shirley hears this!"

I was a long way from Hattiesburg, Mississippi.

Sometimes, things happen, and you fleetingly have a thought, "Wow! That's a possibility." I never had that thought in this case. It never crossed my mind that morning — not even as a fantasy — that before the day was over, I, Walter E. Massey, would be named Chairman of the Bank of America, the largest bank in the United States.

Indeed, I had no idea that this day would be the beginning of one of the most hectic, frustrating, yet ultimately rewarding years of my life.

CHAPTER THREE
HATTIESBURG

I couldn't wait to surprise Shirley with the news that I was the new chairman of the board of Bank of America. *Me!* A black kid who cut classes and played hooky in an unflinchingly segregated town in Mississippi!

After my election, still, in a haze of excitement and disbelief, I rushed out of the meeting to fly home. I started to call Shirley on the way to the airport, only to find out that the battery in my old flip phone had died.

Really? At a time like this!

The flight to Chicago took about an hour and a half. I was flying commercial. I marveled at the thought that this would be my last commercial flight for Bank of America. As chairman, I would have one of the bank's fleet of eight planes at my disposal. Solely for bank-related use, of course. The bank was very strict about not using its planes for non-bank purposes.

By the time I arrived home that evening, Shirley had already heard all about my sudden advancement. Before I could say a word, she blurted out, sounding incredulous, "I heard it on CNN!" and hugged me tightly.

So much for my surprise! The bank had issued an announcement immediately after the meeting. I knew there was a press release, but I had not seen it. I didn't think it would be published so soon. But I should have known it would be. We were in the middle of a crisis. The press, and certainly Wall Street, was waiting to hear what we were going to do. The slightest change in the condition of the bank would be big news. I was just not used to being in the news like that.

Shirley was as shocked as I was. Friends and colleagues from all over the country had been calling with congratulations. Even our two sons called, impressed, and *they* were accustomed to milestone events in our lives, like that time I phoned home, breathless with excitement, from Air Force One, on the way to Coretta Scott King's funeral in 2006; or when I sat next to Queen Elizabeth II, trying hard to stop trembling in awe, at a small dinner at the U.S. ambassador's residence in London to which President George W. Bush had invited us.

"I saw Dad on television. Wow! Chairman of the Bank of America!" my older son, Keith, gushed. It didn't take long for his sardonic sense of humor to kick in. "Can I get a loan, Dad?"

My younger son, Eric, phoned from Amsterdam. He'd gone there for graduate studies and never left. "This sounds fantastic, Dad. I just saw it here on the news, in Dutch."

I was pretty calm by then and starting to feel good about being elected chairman. It was real, and it was a wonderful thing. Yes, Shirley and I had planned our retirement in delightful detail. I had retired as the ninth president of Morehouse College in the spring of 2007, and in a sense, Shirley had retired from Morehouse with me. She became First Lady of the college when I began my presidency in 1995, and she'd thrown herself into her ladyship with her usual civic zeal. Even before we moved to Atlanta, she took a trip there to check things out: the secretaries and various assistants I would be working with, the people we would have to interact with, where we would live, tax issues, and so forth. She is an experienced bookkeeper, having started out in the profession at Playboy Enterprises when she had just turned twenty-years-old.

She argued that the president's home had to be on the campus, instead of off-campus where it was at the time because the students lived *on* campus. That meant selling the off-campus house and building a brand new one on campus. Shirley promptly put herself on the relevant committee to make that happen. She became president of the Morehouse Auxiliary and spearheaded the Morehouse College Beautification Committee.

In our retirement plans, we would keep an apartment in Atlanta but re-establish our main residence in Chicago's Hyde Park, where we had lived on and off for years. Hyde Park is where Shirley grew up and where we were married. We would see more of our friends, travel, relax on Cape Cod where we had a summer home, and spend more time with our sons and two grandchildren. I would keep working on corporate and philanthropic boards — McDonald's, the Andrew W. Mellon Foundation, and others — even though the rules on retirement age would soon force me to resign from some.

I was busy, engaged in things, but I figured my Bank of America chairmanship would fit right in. It might require a day and a half per week, a couple of days at most. From serving on the boards of BP, McDonald's, and Motorola — all of which had non-executive chairmen — I had an idea of what the job required. I would preside over board meetings, help to set the board's agenda and establish committees, represent the bank externally as requested by senior management, meet and speak with shareholders, and make sure that information flowed between management and the board.

Chairman of Bank of America! It's the sort of title a person gets introduced with when they go into places! Yes, this was a wonderful thing.

Little did I know what awaited me.

By now, Shirley was calling people. I could hear her in the kitchen as I took my bags into the den. "Did you hear? Did you hear?" She called everyone we knew from coast to coast, and people from all over called us. Phone calls kept coming in. We talked with a number of people, but I wasn't yet in the mood to brag. The magnitude of my new status was still sinking in.

We wanted to catch the announcement on the evening news, so we kept the TV in the kitchen on and kept changing channels, flicking through the news. We live in a historic and elegant Art Deco co-op building right on Lake Michigan. Our kitchen is rather small, so Shirley usually sits at, or sets the table, which is just big enough for two, while I cook. I do most of the cooking, just as our sons do. It's a family thing.

Finally, there it was!

"Bank of America announced today that Walter Massey, a long-time board member, will be the new bank chairman."

The news went on to say that I was not a banker but an academic and that some considered me an unusual choice. Later editions of the news were more fulsome. They seemed to have researched my background and now commented that I had a great deal of board experience and so my choice was reasonable.

Wow! Now, what do I do? How do I celebrate? I'm chairman of Bank of America. Should we break out the champagne? Should we go out? What does one do when something like this happens? In the end, we did break out the champagne that night and continued to talk about what it meant. And the phone kept ringing, which was nice. Old friends whom we hadn't heard from in a long time called from all over the country.

Later, lying in bed together, it was difficult to calm down and sleep. My thoughts spiraled back to my childhood. They will be so proud of me back in Hattiesburg! I imagined people in my old community saying things like, "Bank of America is everywhere. This is really a big deal." I thought in particular of my oldest and closest childhood friend, Ralph, and our teachers and our classmates. I wondered if some of the white people I used to work for were still alive. What would they think now?

As a teenager, I was driven to escape the oppressive racial atmosphere I grew up in. I said as much in 1980, at the inauguration of Governor William Winter in Jackson, Mississippi. I was participating in a panel of prominent Mississippians, including novelist Eudora Welty. I was the director of the U.S. Department of Energy's Argonne National Laboratory. A reporter for the *Clarion-Ledger* interviewed me after the panel discussion, asking, "Dr. Massey, to what do you ascribe your success in life? What drove you to have such ambition?" Without thinking, I said, "I wanted to get out of Mississippi." This wasn't the answer the reporter expected or even appreciated, and my remarks appeared in the newspaper the next day in bold headlines.

And yet, even though I had wanted to get away from Hattiesburg, I really wanted the people back there to know all that I had accomplished, that one of their own was the chairman of the largest bank in America.

CHAPTER FOUR

THE NORMALCY OF FAMILY, FRIENDS, AND SCHOOL

I was born in Hattiesburg in 1938 and, as strange as it may seem, I think of my childhood as being very happy, despite the rigid segregation of the time and our modest living.

My earliest memories are of the backyard at my maternal grandmother's home. Grandmother Betty — Momma, as I called her — made soap in a big, black kettle, the same one she used to boil our clothes. The soap was a combination of lye, ash, and I'm not sure what else.

We often saw rabbits in her yard. Of course, we always had to watch out for snakes, but they were mostly harmless garter snakes, unlike the rattlesnakes that infested the bunkers at Camp Shelby, the army base outside of town where we went hunting when I was older. And there was a big pecan tree in the yard next door that spilled nuts over into our yard.

I was in my grandmother's backyard the first time I remember seeing my father. He had just come home in his Army uniform on furlough, I think. I had seen pictures of him when I was a young child, but this was the first time I remember seeing him in person.

The man I call my father here, Almor Massey, wasn't my biological father. He married my mother when I was two,

23

adopted me, and raised me as his son. My parents never tried to hide the fact that my biological father, Chester Gaines, was my mother's college boyfriend. She became pregnant with me in 1937 while attending Alcorn College. She'd had to drop out of school. She and Chester remained friends for life. He moved to Detroit after the war and married a local girl, Bernetta Lanier. They always wrote, sent gifts, and often visited us in the summer.

My mother, father, and I were living then at my grandmother's house. It was a small house, though it seemed large to me, as did our backyard. There were four rooms: a bedroom where my grandmother and I each had a bed; a living room; a bedroom where my parents slept beside my brother, Al, in his crib when he came along; and a kitchen. We didn't have an indoor toilet or bath at the time. We did have an outhouse, and I took baths in a big, round galvanized tub. I recall later being very proud that our house wasn't a "shotgun" house (three rooms, one behind the other, that you could see straight through from front to back as if you were looking down an empty shotgun barrel).

Like most streets in our neighborhood, the street we lived on, Scooba Street, was a dirt road with no sidewalks. When it rained, the road turned muddy, and streams of water ran along the sides of it. I loved playing in those streams and racing my little make-shift boats.

My father was raised in Perkinston, a tiny farming community about 20 miles south of Hattiesburg, by his Uncle Buster and Aunt Clara. Al, who was younger than me by four years, and I spent our summers with them on their large piece of farmland and woodland. They had horses we could ride, as well as cows, hogs, pigs, and chickens, and a creek that ran through the property where we caught fish. Uncle Buster and Aunt Clara also grew sugar cane, and we'd make fresh syrup using an old grinding wheel that was powered by their mule. Al and I, along with our cousins, would drink the fresh cane juice and get horribly sick. But we had wonderful times on the farm.

It's where I first learned to hunt, shooting squirrels and rabbits with my .410 shotgun.

The only problem was the lack of indoor toilets. It was very dark and scary to use the outhouse at night. We had no electricity on the farm in the early days. As an adult, I once revisited the farm and was amazed by how close the outhouse was to the main house. It seemed so far when I was a boy.

The highlight of the summer was harvest time. We would all pitch in to pick the corn and put up the berries, fruits, and vegetables. We'd make cane syrup, slaughter the animals, and cure or smoke the bacon, ham, and sausages. Relatives from up North would join us around harvest time, and they'd take home food to Chicago, Gary, and Detroit.

My mother, Essie, was a primary school teacher, and she later became an elementary school principal. Named after her grandfather, Essex, she was a curious, energetic, restless person. There was always something new happening with her. She had a different home venture every summer — a kindergarten one year, a beauty parlor, the next — and vegetable gardens, chickens, and new flower beds every spring. She was a good seamstress, and she'd buy clothes for Al and me, irrespective of size. She would simply re-sew them to make them fit.

My mother liked books and music, and I learned to read at a very early age, possibly before I turned three. I can't remember not reading. My grandmother taught me how. I recall reading on her lap. My mother always had books around. There were simplified versions of the classics, including the Greek myths and Biblical stories, and a multi-volume encyclopedia that must have been sold by some door-to-door salesman. We had no TV set until around 1950. My mother probably had the greatest influence on my life. She had gone to college to become a schoolteacher, and though she didn't graduate, she earned a teaching certificate, as many colored teachers did in those days. Her sister, my Aunt Ruth, also got a teaching certificate without finishing four years of college. There had been teachers in our family since the early 1900s.

One of my mother's first teaching jobs was in a one-room schoolhouse in a small farming community outside Hattiesburg. Her pupils ranged in age from kindergarten to fourth or fifth grade. Sometimes, my mother would take me to that schoolhouse with her, and though I was younger than many of her students, I participated in the room's activities. The school year, in that small community of farmers, lasted only about six months for coloreds. When it was time to pick cotton, the colored schools closed so that the children could join in with the picking.

Much later, when I was developing a course for science teachers at Brown University, I recalled how my mother managed to teach all those kids in that one-room schoolhouse. I adopted the same method of peer-to-peer teaching she had used.

People around town, especially women, would say things to me like, "You look just like your daddy; so good-looking." They were speaking of my biological father, Chester. I do not know if Almor heard these things. But if he did, I imagine they must have bothered him because he was such a proud man and really did think of me as his son, not as a stepson or adopted son. He was a very good dad. He taught me to hunt and fish and do all sorts of boy things. I learned to drive at 11, though my foot could barely reach the clutch, and I had my first shotgun, a .410 when I was 12 or so.

Almor worked hard. In addition to his job at Hercules Power Company, a local chemical plant, he sold insurance on weekends and liked to dress in a shirt and tie when he did so. He didn't drink, and he carried himself with dignity around both whites and Negroes. His attitude and demeanor were one of calm, respectability, and dogged independence. He was careful in dealing with whites and cautioned us to be careful around them, too. He didn't demean himself, and he never seemed afraid or intimidated by white people, but neither was he confrontational. He knew which lines not to cross.

This may have been due to two factors. One, his Uncle Buster, was a fairly prosperous landowner and farmer and was treated with a certain amount of respect by his neighboring white farmers. That didn't stop them, though, from conspiring for years to get part of his land, but Uncle Buster held on until he died and willed the land to his heirs.

Two, he was a long-time employee at Hercules. Hercules was a unique institution in Hattiesburg. It was probably unique in the United States, period. It was founded in 1912 as a result of a court-mandated divestiture from the DuPont Corporation. The Hattiesburg plant opened in 1920 and became the most important industrial enterprise in the area, employing chemists and engineers, as well as skilled and manual laborers. Given today's attitudes toward unions in the South, it is remarkable that Hercules was also a union shop and that blacks were part of the union.

Enlightened (or profit-driven) northern white management, along with a unique local white union leader, Hank Dunagin, created an environment where colored employees could earn a fairly decent living and acquire job skills that allowed them to advance. Dunagin assured black workers they would not lose their jobs by pursuing their legal right to vote — an extraordinary position for a white supervisor to take at that time in Mississippi.

My father was also a deacon at our church, Sweet Pilgrim Baptist Church, which was only two houses away from our house. Everyone in our community, and probably in the whole town, attended church on Sundays, and often on Wednesdays as well, for Bible lessons. There were Methodists in town and a few 'sanctified' people (now called Pentecostals), but I don't recall knowing any Catholics, Episcopalians, or Presbyterians. We were almost all Baptists. I disliked sitting in church for long sermons, but I enjoyed reading the Bible, and I was good at Bible verse contests. These were hard games. You'd be told the chapter and verse in a certain book of the Bible — Isaiah 43:2, for instance — and had to recite the verse from memory.

On Sundays after church, we'd have fried chicken for lunch. This was a big treat, and as I got older, I was selected to choose the chicken from the yard and then catch it and kill it. This wasn't as easy as it sounds because the roosters were very protective and aggressive. Some people caught chickens and killed them by chopping their heads off, but our preferred method was to hold the chicken by the head and ring its neck.

Both my grandfathers worked at Mississippi Southern College, the white-only college that is now the University of Southern Mississippi. My grandfather on Chester's side, Richard Gaines, worked on the grounds in a variety of jobs for forty-five years and knew the heating and plumbing systems so well that they called him "The Walking Blueprint." My mother's father was a cook at the college, and I remember him bringing home food from the school. We always had plenty of food. My father and uncles hunted and fished, and we always had kitchen gardens. Almor also had access to the company commissary at Hercules, so we could shop there, with discounts for groceries. I loved going to the commissary and getting canned goods. Ironically, I much preferred cans of Green Giant peas to those fresh from our gardens. I still do.

Because both my parents had regular jobs, before long, we moved out of my grandmother's house and into our own house two blocks away, next door to my Uncle Ed, my mother's brother. Ed had seven children, and two of them, Tommy and Jerry, were about my age — one a year older, the other a year younger. The three of us were very close.

As children, we played outdoors until dark. We could do so because in our neighborhood, we were safe and a little supervised, even if our parents didn't have an eye on us. All the adults looked after all the children; every adult had a right to correct every child. And, of course, many adults and children were related. I am sure that the feeling of freedom this created — to explore, to play, to invent games and activities — was a major factor in my having a happy childhood.

I always had lots of friends, cousins, and playmates, but I do recall being quite happy to play alone. I liked to read and listen to records or the radio. Sometimes I would overhear my mother's friends say to her, "Peeka sure likes to read, doesn't he?" (To this day, I have not been able to trace the source of my nickname.) "I guess he's going to be a teacher like you." As I got older, I would think to myself; *I don't want to be a teacher. I want to do something different.*

My best friend was Ralph Woullard, whose backyard bordered ours. The Woullards were a prominent colored family in Hattiesburg. Ralph's grandfather was a well-to-do preacher and pastor. Ralph and I were almost constant companions from primary school until I left Hattiesburg to attend Morehouse College after the 10th grade. We walked to school, and we loved to play hooky. We would sneak out of school to play or, on rare occasions, we'd go to the movies at the Lomo Theater and sit in the balcony.

It says something about the times, the neighborhood, and the sense of community that our being neither in school nor at home, caused no panic on our teachers' or parents' parts, and no fear on our part.

One day, my mother appeared at our school. I was probably in the third grade at the time. My teacher had asked her if I'd been sick since I'd missed so many days at school. That's when my mother learned I'd been playing hooky. She made a switch from the small branches of a bush or tree and whipped me out of school and through the neighborhood, all the way home. My schoolmates laughed and jeered at the spectacle as all our neighbors looked on from their porches, smiling.

Being reprimanded at my mother's hand was publicly humiliating, but it wasn't enough to keep me from skipping school. This practice would seem not to bode well for my future. But I really liked to learn, and I found school fun and interesting. I always enjoyed reading, and especially doing number exercises. I do not recall ever being pushed or admonished to do homework. I liked doing it, and that was something my mother took for granted. But in my boyish world, school was not a priority. Ralph and I kept cutting classes and playing hooky all the way through elementary school and even high school. However, in high school, we cut class mostly to practice in a rhythm and blues group Ralph and I, along with some other classmates, had formed.

Our band was called the Blue Gardenias. I played alto saxophone, and Ralph played baritone sax. We were quite good — good enough to play in the area's adult nightclubs. Once, when I stayed the night at Ralph's house, we snuck out his back window with our saxophones and rode our bicycles out to a club to play in the band. Hattiesburg was a small town, so our parents quickly learned about our gig. Later on, they would come to see us perform and were very proud of how well we played and how much the audience liked us.

Like everything else in Hattiesburg, the public schools were starkly segregated. But I never felt deprived. We had excellent, dedicated teachers, and their effectiveness was verified by my first year at Morehouse College and beyond. However, after the U.S. Supreme Court ruled in *Brown v. Board of Education* that laws allowing racial segregation in public schools were unconstitutional, we discovered that our books, supplies, and practically everything else in our schools, were inferior to those in white schools. Our buildings and facilities were nowhere near as appealing as those of the white schools, which I often passed but never entered. Our teachers made up for this discrimination. I was well-prepared for college.

In 1950, a new school, Royal Street High School, was built in our neighborhood, only a few blocks from where we lived. It was actually a combined middle school, junior high, and high school, starting in the seventh grade. To us, it was wonderful. It was newer than Hattiesburg High, the white school. We had a large playground for athletics and band practice, a nice, new auditorium, and many other excellent features. It's now clear that Royal Street High, like other new schools for Negroes built at around the same time, was not a goodwill gesture of the Hattiesburg school system, but part of Mississippi's preparations to defend its "separate but equal" policy, which the Supreme Court had established in its *Plessy v. Ferguson* decision in 1896.

In the fourth grade, before Royal St. High School was built, I attended Eureka, which was an elementary, as well as middle and high school on the other side of town from where we lived. It was a very long walk, so Ralph, my other friends, and I mostly took the public bus. Of course, we sat in the back of the bus in the colored seats and were careful not to do anything to offend the bus drivers who were white. But when we pulled the cord for our stop, sometimes the drivers would deliberately drive several blocks past our stop, letting us off in the poor white neighborhood where kids would throw rocks at us. As I recall, we were not afraid of them, and sometimes, we would throw rocks back.

I was always a good pupil in school, but I didn't think of myself among the school's outstanding students. After all, Ralph and I played hooky so often. We were mostly absorbed in our music. Imagine my surprise when I was included in a group chosen to go to Jackson, the state capital, to take an exam for a scholarship that the Ford Foundation was offering.

A few months later, I was playing ball in the street with some friends when I saw my mother speeding toward us and waving a large envelope out of the car window. We all wondered what had her so excited. The envelope was addressed to me, and it was from Morehouse College in Atlanta. The Ford Foundation had awarded me a four-year scholarship that included early admission to Morehouse. I was the only student in Mississippi to get one of the scholarships. But I was still only in the 10th grade, and I hadn't yet turned sixteen. The family did much soul-searching over whether I should accept the offer. Most on my mother's side had attended college, but almost all of them had gone to Mississippi schools: Tougaloo, Jackson State, or Alcorn. We all expected I would go to college, too, but not so soon, and not in Atlanta, where we didn't know a soul.

My father worried about my leaving home at such a young age. My mother was encouraging. She had high ambitions for herself and for me, and I think she saw my early admission to college as a fulfillment of her own aspirations. I was nervous about going, but excited and happy when the family finally agreed that I should go. I was a "big man" in our community now, on my way to Atlanta. Even the white people we knew or worked for seemed impressed.

Bound for Morehouse in the summer of 1954, just months after the *Brown v. Board of Education* decision, I rode The Southerner, / a beautiful, silver express train, to Atlanta. As Hattiesburg faded in the distance, I did not look back.

CHAPTER FIVE
I YEARNED FOR MORE

Growing up in Hattiesburg in the 1940s and 1950s, I saw a town as rigidly segregated as the rest of Mississippi. Everything was labeled 'white' or 'colored.' Coloreds, as we were called then, rode in the back of the bus and had to use 'colored' drinking fountains, 'colored' restrooms, and 'colored' everything, it seemed. The only place we could sit in a movie theater was in the 'colored' balcony. Being 'uppity' with whites was a serious matter, and we learned at a very early age that looking directly at white girls was considered a dangerous risk-taking.

Yet, the racial environment and colored-white relationships were more complex than these simple taboos imply. There were whites who were not hostile to blacks. Probably all whites were segregationists, but certainly, not all were in favor of lynchings, bombings, and other violent acts against coloreds. In our small-town Southern manner, relationships that were cordial and helpful could develop across racial lines, but, of course, always within certain boundaries.

Even before I encountered segregated drinking fountains and shopping facilities in downtown Hattiesburg, I knew about white people, mostly through stories my grandmother, mother, grandfather, uncles, and aunts would tell about the people they worked for. In their telling, there were different kinds of white

33

people. There were the poor whites, or 'white trash,' some of whom lived not far from us; the 'good' whites, such as the Morrises and the Stillmans, who owned a nearby grocery store that hired my older cousins; and the distant white bosses, such as Mr. Tatum, who owned Tatum Woods and the Saw Mill, and who "really controlled things," as people would say. With the abundance of pine trees in this region, the economy then was based largely on the lumber industry. Even now, the region is known as Piney Woods.

Grandmother Betty worked as a domestic servant for the Morrises. She was paid very little, we thought — two dollars a day and bus fare — but she always said the Morrises were kind and thoughtful employers, given the time and place. I recall going to work with her when I was three or four and playing regularly with the Morris children, a girl and a boy about my age. This was great fun because they had a big house and a big yard and lots of toys. I also recall vividly, even now, the day my grandmother told me I could no longer go to work with her. The Morrises thought I was getting too old to be playing with their daughter. I wasn't yet five. Later, it would dawn on me that although we played together in the backyard and ate together in the kitchen, I had never been in the rest of the Morrises' home, and I had never entered through the front door.

So, I was beginning to understand that we colored people were different. We lived on the other side of the railroad tracks, literally, and we didn't play with white girls. But I had not yet experienced real racial hostility. The first time I did was not long after my banishment from the Morrises' backyard before I even entered school. My grandmother had a beautiful German shepherd named Lady. I am told that even when I was a toddler, Lady would babysit me by barking away strangers or visitors from my playpen. A local policeman — white, as they all were — approached my grandmother several times about buying Lady. Each time he asked, my grandmother still said she would not sell her dog.

One day, I saw Lady lying on a garbage heap across from Stillman's grocery, caked in blood, with maggots crawling over her. I do not recall if I just happened upon her, or if someone took me there — perhaps my cousin, Eddie James, who worked at Stillman's — to show me what had happened to Lady. I learned later that the policeman who wanted to buy her, along with his pals, lured Lady to the garbage site about a block from our house and shot her in the head.

For years I forgot or suppressed the memory of Lady's death. What did it mean to me then — that things happened in life beyond our control, tragedies even? That there were evil, white people, whose power to do bad things, to commit atrocities — I certainly did not know that word then — was pretty much unlimited? I'm not sure. But looking back, I believe that this incident, especially because I didn't think about it until I began to write this memoir, must have had a profound effect on my development.

Still, it didn't seem to mar the overall happiness of my childhood. The colored community in Hattiesburg was very close. But Hattiesburg was also large enough to have more and less prosperous colored neighborhoods. These two sides of the town had somewhat visible economic and educational differences. Yet, only a very few families were thought to be rich or well-to-do. The heads of these families were Reverend Woullard, my best friend Ralph's grandfather; Dr. Smith, who owned the drugstore and lunchroom; Mr. Nathaniel Burger, the high school principal, who had a status for reasons other than money; and a few nightclub owners and bootleggers. Schoolteachers and preachers were especially respected, and my mother, being a teacher, put us in the "respected" group.

Hattiesburg was less overtly and blatantly racially oppressive than much of the northern and western parts of Mississippi, at least when I grew up there. Rigid segregation and racist barriers existed and were scrupulously adhered to, but there were no large cotton plantations and few vestiges of sharecropping in this part of the state. Even though some of the state's most vociferous white segregationists, Theodore Bilbo, for example, came from the Hattiesburg area, we still felt better off than colored people in the Delta, where the large slave-holding estates had been located. As I noted, my father's Uncle Buster owned several acres of prime farmland and timber groves, and we knew many other colored landowners.

The scariest things about whites, more than the day-to-day realities I faced, was the unpredictability of interactions with them. The stories I was told about things that happened to other colored people — as at Richburg Hill, a legendary place not far from where we lived, where lynchings were said to have occurred — made us understand that even in our day and time, blacks could still be beaten, shot, or lynched without warning.

Even the "good" whites were unpredictable. My first real boyhood job was as the cook's helper at Marco Courts, a new motel owned by two white women, Margaret and Cora. It seemed to be common knowledge, even in Mississippi in the early 1950s, that they were a gay couple. Before long, I was promoted from cook's helper to a better job, bellhop. I got to carry the luggage of couples who struck me as glamorous and sophisticated, and I dreamed of being like them someday. Plus, I got tips.

Ironically, Miss Cora, who managed the motel and restaurant, was one of the most important early influences in my life. She owned a big pink-and-white Lincoln Continental convertible, and sometimes she let me drive it home so I could ferry some of the black 'help' to work the next day. There were even afternoons when I'd drive it to take the day's cash to the bank downtown. I became known to blacks and whites around town as Miss Cora's trusted ward. As a bellhop, I spent most of my time standing next to Miss Cora at the front desk. We talked about my school and my work, and she gave me advice on how to give excellent service and interact with guests to get better tips.

I liked Miss Cora and felt she wanted the best for me. I even harbored a fantasy that she might finance my college education, though I can't recall where I got such an idea. I never heard Miss Cora say anything racially derogatory. She treated all her employees pretty much the same, whether black or white. Her most trusted employee, in fact, was the head cook and de facto boss of the restaurant kitchen, my cousin Frenchie.

On May 17, 1954, the U.S. Supreme Court handed down its unanimous decision in *Brown v. Board of Education*, ruling that the nation's schools should be desegregated. I was standing next to Miss Cora as she read the headline in the Hattiesburg American. "We're not going to let coloreds go to school with whites," she said. "This is horrible."

I was crushed. Though Miss Cora's reaction to integration was devastating to me, it did not take away all that I had learned from her on the job. She gave me responsibility and instilled in me a work ethic that I carried throughout my life. She also helped me learn how to work with other people — both black and white.

One consequence of living in such a rigidly segregated society was that white people weren't an everyday concern for us unless we worked for them or they lived nearby. To be sure, there was always the danger that some gesture, comment, or action on our part could trigger a violent reaction. White girls, in particular, were treacherous terrain. In my first part-time job — a carhop at a drive-in restaurant that served ice cream and hot dogs — I learned when white girls paid me, to put their change on the tray and not let my hands touch theirs. Some white girls would try to get us to extend our hands for payment so that we'd touch them. But there was always the fear that they did this just so they could claim we'd flirted with them. A charge like that could be deadly — literally. I was just eleven or twelve at the time, basking in the validation of my maturity from having obligations and responsibilities of a job, but I was already very aware of these dangers.

When I tell people that in spite of all this, I had an overwhelmingly happy childhood in rigidly segregated Mississippi, many are incredulous. "How could this happen?" they seem to be saying, or "I can't imagine myself being happy in such circumstances." Sometimes, I sense they are thinking, "Well, you must be suppressing some deep-seated memories and emotions," or "You would have been much happier if you had been white."

Because of these reactions, I have often wondered if all the white kids were happier than I was. Were the Morris kids happier than Ralph and my cousins? Did they turn out to be better people? More successful people? Did they have a larger impact on society? I don't think so. What then, was it about my childhood that allowed me and others to grow up feeling good in such a hostile environment? A lot goes back to my mother, my grandmother — people would tell me I was her favorite, even though she had several grandchildren — my uncles, cousins, and neighbors. The fact is, growing up, I always felt special, and I always felt loved.

Still, I did have a desire to leave Mississippi and see the world. This was motivated mostly by what I had read about or heard about from relatives who had traveled or lived elsewhere, especially those from 'up North.'

When I was around ten or eleven, our family traveled to Chicago on occasion to visit relatives. These experiences were very mixed for me. Our relatives in Chicago were, for the most part, poor — or at least they seemed to be. They lived in small apartments far from the bustling, lively parts of the city, and they did not appear to be better off or happier for being 'up North.' During these visits to Chicago, though, I got my first taste of the big city. I would take the electric streetcar downtown to State Street and marvel at the neon lights, burlesque clubs, arcades, and glamorous people.

The exception to my experience of northern poverty was my mother's best friend, who was also named Essie, and her husband, Bryce Simms, who lived in Gary, Indiana. Gary was a prosperous community with nice homes, tree-lined streets, and beautiful sidewalks where I could ride my small bicycle. Bryce had a large jazz record collection, and I would sit and listen for hours. I loved visiting the Simms.

In the summer of 1955, I made my first trip to Detroit to visit my biological father and stepmother. I traveled all the way from Hattiesburg on a Greyhound bus. Of course, the bus was segregated, with Negroes sitting in the back. There were no restrooms on that bus, and until we reached Ohio, all the rest stops for food and toilets were segregated as well. It was in Detroit that I first encountered Negroes who were positively wealthy. I recall that when I saw the big houses on Chicago Boulevard and Boston Boulevard, I was amazed that they belonged to Negroes. It was even more shocking to see Negroes with chauffeurs. These rich people tended to be ministers, doctors, businessmen, and high-level numbers operators.

Was it just luck that I survived life in Hattiesburg relatively unscathed? In part, I suppose. But, I believe the larger reason I remained safe is that I was swaddled in a loving, supportive family environment. I was totally unaware of efforts to secure rights for blacks, which helps to explain some of the protective aurae I felt as a child. My mother and aunt were schoolteachers, my grandfathers both worked at the local college, Mississippi Southern, and my father worked at Hercules. All this must have given my family some sense of confidence and some sense of standing, which was reflected in the safety and security I felt as a child.

It is also true; I now realize that I was not satisfied with my 'station' in life. I wanted to live the life I read about in books and saw in movies. The differences between where colored and white people could live, where we could go, shop, eat, or do anything else became more apparent to me as I became a teenager. The life I wanted simply did not exist for me in colored Mississippi, and there were no signs in the early 1950s that this was going to change. So, the only option, if one wanted a different life, was to leave and "go North" as many colored people, including many of my relatives, did.

Had I stayed in Hattiesburg, would I have applied to Mississippi Southern College? I do not think so, even if the school had opened itself to coloreds. MSC was not a particularly prestigious college, even in Mississippi. It was founded in the early 1900s as a 'normal' school, a teacher training institution, and was still primarily a school for teacher education, nursing, and similar practical pursuits. I did not know all this at the time, but I did know that, although MSC had a very beautiful campus and was within walking distance of our neighborhood, its reputation did not match schools like Massachusetts Institute of Technology, the University of Chicago, Michigan, and the like. These were schools I had read about, and I knew that blacks could attend.

The truth is, I did not want to go to college in Mississippi. But if the Morehouse offer had not come along so unexpectedly and early, I might not have had any other choice.

In her March 2019 *New York Times* review of *HATTIESBURG: An American City in Black and White*, by historian William Sturkey, Jennifer Szalai summarizes Hattiesburg as a city engulfed in "the depredations of racial apartheid;" a town whose "white power brokers…sought to maintain an unyielding, repressive racial order."

When I retired from the board of trustees for the Mellon Foundation in 2009, I received an email from a fellow trustee, Taylor Reverly, a white Southerner who was then president of the College of William and Mary. Taylor wrote: "Walter, it has been a pleasure working with you. I will miss our interactions. I have found it remarkable that, growing up when and where you did in the deep South, you manage to exhibit so much grace and so little bitterness in your life and in your interactions with everyone…"

I do not think I am unique in my feelings or behavior. Many of my colleagues, friends, and relatives of my generation grew up similarly. We do not harbor bitterness toward whites; at least I don't think so. What we do feel is a sense of loss for how much more we all might have become. Certainly, I have a profound regret that our parents did not have the opportunity to be all they could have been. But I also feel sorry for all those young whites who grew up in an environment that made many of them hateful, violent, racist individuals. Their lives have also been stunted.

From my perspective now, looking backward and forward, I suspect that one day soon, it is going to be much more embarrassing and personally painful to admit to being a descendant of slave owners, than to be a descendent of slaves.

I have often thought how different my life might be had I remained to finish high school in Hattiesburg, and had I remained in Mississippi after 1954. I certainly would not have advanced as fast academically if I had spent two more years in high school rather than two years in college. I probably would have been caught up in the burgeoning Civil Rights Movement, and who knows, may have stayed on in Hattiesburg.

I also think about the traits, characteristics, attitudes, behaviors, and beliefs that growing up in Hattiesburg during that period implanted in me. Three things stand out: first, one should try very hard not to let external surroundings and circumstances be the primary determinant of one's attitudes and behavior, because hard work, intestinal fortitude, and persistence (I know this sounds very trite) will carry a person a long way in life. Second, family and friends are important, as is an openness to look for and accept help and guidance, whatever the source, whatever the race from whence it may come. And, finally, for me, the resilience, creativity, and persistence of my mother clearly had a lifelong influence.

Had I *not* grown up in Hattiesburg, would I have become the man deemed most suitable for the role of chairman of the Bank of America in its time of crisis?

Chapter Six

A CALL FROM CROATIA
AND THE FUN BEGINS

My euphoria about my new position didn't last long.

The day after I was elected chairman, I got a call from Charles (Chad) Gifford, one of our board members. Chad was the CEO of FleetBoston Financial Corporation — Fleet Bank — when Bank of America bought it in 2004. Chad was a good guy, a very good guy. He was one of the people I thought could become chair. In fact, when we purchased Fleet, he *did* become chair for a year, but that was part of the purchase agreement. Since he was chairman and CEO of Fleet, we would elect him chairman of Bank of America with the understanding that he would serve in that capacity for just a year. He would go through the merger, and then Ken would resume the seat of the chair a year later.

Chad was in Croatia and had missed Wednesday's meetings. He called me at my home Thursday afternoon, around four o'clock. I was about to leave to play tennis.

I had not learned to play tennis until I was in my late twenties, which, for an avid tennis player, is considered very late in life. But I fell in love with the game. It combined so many things I liked: vigorous exercise, strategic thinking, friendly competition, and an international social environment in which

I could always make new friends. Most important, perhaps, was that tennis helped me to control stress and lower my high blood pressure.

"Walter, well, Mr. Chairman. How do you like that!"

Chad had a sense of humor and joked that if he had been at the board meeting, he would have cast the only vote against me. Then, becoming serious, he said, "Walter, do you have time to take a phone call from someone at the Fed? One of my colleagues at the Fed in Boston asked me to give you a call. He says you should speak with Kevin Warsh."

"Sure."

"He'll call in fifteen minutes. So, is this a good number for you?"

I assured him it was, and we hung up. I was puzzled. Why did Chad have to call me all the way from Croatia to deliver a message from a friend of his at the Boston Fed that I should connect with Kevin Warsh? It seemed so circuitous. Why couldn't Kevin Warsh call me directly? I never learned why.

Fifteen minutes after I hung up with Chad, Kevin called.

I'd never met Kevin Warsh, but I knew his name. He was a governor of the Federal Reserve and the right-hand man of Fed Chairman Ben Bernanke. He was a "wunderkind" in financial circles. He had worked at Morgan Stanley and then became a special assistant to President George W. Bush for economic policy. When he was appointed to the Federal Reserve Board in 2006 at age 35, he was the youngest appointee in the history of the Fed.

"First of all, congratulations," he said. "And congratulations from the chairman. I want you to know we think this is a good choice, and we are behind you on this."

At the time, Bank of America was under all kinds of scrutiny. Kevin Warsh was the person centrally involved when, after we purchased Merrill Lynch, we tried to get out of the deal. We tried to get out of it with what's called a MAC — Material Adverse Change — which is a provision in merger and acquisition contracts that allows the acquiring party to back out of the deal if there is a major change in the entity being acquired. When we learned of the huge losses Merrill was piling up in the fourth quarter of 2008, Ken Lewis informed the Fed that we were considering invoking the MAC. Ultimately, after tense negotiations with the Treasury and the Federal Reserve, the bank decided not to invoke the MAC. Kevin Warsh was Ben Bernanke's point person in those negotiations.

So, I knew who Kevin Warsh was.

"I want to give you a message," he said to me on the phone. "You need to know that the message comes from the OCC, the FDIC, and the Treasury, as well as the Fed."

He didn't say, "You *should* know." He said, "You *need* to know." So, this was serious. Really serious. It was imperative I heard the message that had been discussed with other agencies. And this was just the *first* day! Barely twenty-four hours since my election as chairman.

"Yes," I responded.

He continued, "Well, you're going to get a call from the president of the Federal Reserve Bank in Richmond."

"Okay."

The Federal Reserve Bank in Richmond, Virginia, is one of the regional banks of the Federal Reserve System, our central banking system. Depending on where the headquarters of a bank is located, that bank is subject to oversight by the Fed in that specific region. The Richmond Fed supervised the Bank of America. Almost every other major U.S. bank, except Wells Fargo, is in New York, and they're under the New York Fed.

Warsh said, "You need to listen very carefully to what he says." He explained that certain things had to be done at the bank, and Jeff Lacker, president of the Richmond Fed, was the person to speak to. He stated that Lacker had the full backing of the Federal Reserve, the Treasury, the Federal Deposit Insurance Corporation (FDIC), and the Office of the Comptroller of the Currency (OCC), so I should take very seriously whatever he told me.

He spoke in a warm, cordial tone. There was no hint whatsoever of harshness or threat. It was all conversational. I was to learn later, after many talks with him, that this was his style even when delivering unpleasant messages.

He congratulated me once more and hung up.

Fifteen minutes later, Lacker called.

"Dr. Massey?"

"Yes."

"This is Jeffrey Lacker, president of the Richmond Fed. I'd like you to come down."

It was clear that "I'd *like* you to come down," did not mean, "I *hope you would* come down." Jeff Lacker had given me an order.

"I'd like you to come to Richmond to meet with us because we have some information to convey, and it's very important that you hear it in person."

"Okay."

"Also, it would be good if you could bring three or four other directors with you because, when you deliver the message we give you, it would be good if other directors could help you to make your report to the board."

"Okay. Is there anyone you would recommend?"

"No, this is up to you. But you should bring some people who are bankers who have banking experience."

I knew which board members had banking and finance experience, so I was able to come up with one name right away.

"What about Chad Gifford?" I asked. Chad had been CEO of FleetBoston Financial, a major bank. I thought he would be back from Croatia by the time we had the meeting.

"Yes, that's a good choice," Lacker said.

"Maybe Tom May?" I suggested. Thomas J. May was chairman of our Audit Committee and chairman and CEO of NSTAR, an electric utility headquartered in Boston, but he was not a banker.

"I think Tom would be very good," Jeff Lacker said anyway. "He is well respected by the staff, and they have a lot of confidence in him because they interacted with him regularly as chairman of the Audit Committee. Who else would you like to bring?"

Another banker, Frank Bramble, came to mind. Frank was the chief executive of Maryland National Bank when Bank of America acquired it in 2004. I'd always found him to be a thoughtful and perceptive director. I also thought of Charles Rossotti, who had just joined our board from Merrill Lynch's board. He was a former IRS commissioner and businessman, and one of our smartest and hardest-working directors. I mentioned the two names to Lacker.

"Sounds good."

"Okay. When would you like us to be there?"

"Tomorrow afternoon."

What! Tomorrow afternoon? I was pretty much speechless. I'd expected him to say "Monday" at the earliest. I'm in Chicago. I don't have a private plane. I have no idea how to get to Richmond from Chicago.

Aloud, I said, "Four people to get there by tomorrow afternoon? At four or so? Well, I'll try." I was still incredulous.

"It's very important," Lacker said pleasantly.

I turned to Shirley as soon as I got off the phone. Shirley is a former travel agent.

"I need to go to Richmond tomorrow," I said to her.

"Why?"

"'I have a meeting at the Federal Reserve there."

"Are they making the flight arrangements?"

"No, they didn't say so."

"I suppose I could call someone in Charlotte, but I'm not sure the bank is supposed to know about this," I said. "Can you find out about flights?"

When Shirley and I met, she was working in International Reservations for the old TWA airline. She had also worked as a travel agent in Providence when we were at Brown University. She has always handled all of our travel, and even my business travel, because she is so much more experienced and efficient than any executive assistant I ever had. All of my assistants have loved her for this. She relieves them of a burden, and she works well with everyone. She knows all of the airline and travel inside codes, systems, and shortcuts. Sometimes, when she's on the phone making travel arrangements for me or for both of us, she seems to be speaking another language. But the agents on the other end apparently identify with her, and they quickly become "buddies" or "co-conspirators" in trying to figure out what she needs.

Shirley also has the patience that comes with being in the travel business. She can remain on "hold" during a phone call, seemingly forever, doing crossword puzzles while she waits. I get irritable when being put on hold, but Shirley invariably remains polite, chatty, and charming. She knows what the person on the other end is going through and empathizes with them. She is a master at getting deals and special treatment for us.

"What time do you have to be there?" she asked.

"In time for a four o'clock meeting. And remember, Richmond is on Eastern Time."

She flashed me a what-makes-you-think-I'd-forget look as she went into her office. She has an office of her own in our apartment. Its walls are covered with family photographs. It is here that she manages all of our finances and taxes, and keeps our personal records. It is also where she works on her community engagements.

She opened her computer, logged into her phone, and started checking flights. She always seems more relaxed than me in circumstances that call for this kind of logistical maneuvering. I had learned to leave her alone when she began to work, so I went into the den, got on my phone, and started trying to reach Frank Bramble, Charles Rossotti, and Tom May.

I was amazed that I was able to reach all of them as quickly as I did. I told each of them exactly what Kevin Warsh and Jeff Lacker had said. I added nothing, but I was stressed that Lacker said the meeting was very important and that it was critical that we gathered right away. I told Tom to hunt down

Chad Gifford to see if he could join us in the meeting by phone. I knew he and Chad were good friends.

Naturally, they plied me with questions.

"What else did Warsh say, Walter?"

"Did Lacker add anything?"

"Does anyone know Lacker?"

All I could say was that both Warsh and Lacker sounded very serious but not alarmed.

Remarkably, we all managed to arrive at the Richmond Fed at about 3 p.m. on Friday, May 1, fifty-one hours after my chairmanship began. Tom May barely made it from Boston. There was a storm, and he couldn't get a commercial flight, so he called Chad in Croatia, and Chad arranged for a private plane through a board he was a member of and got Tom there on time.

CHAPTER SEVEN
IN THE EYE OF THE FED

The Federal Reserve buildings I knew — in Chicago, New York, Atlanta, and San Francisco — were solid, monumental edifices that resembled city halls or libraries, with their massive columns and broad imposing entrances. The one in Richmond looked like a modern skyscraper that housed commercial offices or apartments. There was nothing arresting about it. It was not located in the center of the city, but in an area of downtown Richmond that boasted what looked like relatively new buildings. I guessed it was the financial district because of the modern SunTrust Bank nearby. When my taxi pulled into the parking lot adjoining the Fed, it took me several minutes to find the front entrance of the building.

My colleagues and I waited in the outer office for a few minutes, talking nervously among ourselves in hushed tones as we tried to divine what was going on and marveling at the fact that all of us had managed to get there — and on time. My mind raced in anticipation of the meeting ahead. I was so taken up with what was coming that I paid little attention to our surroundings, except to observe that they were rather modern in design, with none of the ornate moldings and grand windows I associated with other Fed buildings.

If you ever go to a Seder, when Jewish families observe Passover, you will hear the ritual question, "Why is this night different from all other nights?" I've always taken this to mean, 'why are we here? Why have we gathered? What are we doing here?' That's exactly what we were asking ourselves: Why are we here? We all knew it was serious when Kevin Warsh said he was delivering a message that had been discussed with the other agencies, but I had no idea how serious it was. None of us did. We all were thinking, "What could it be? What are they going to tell us? Do they want us to fire the management? What is so urgent?"

Pretty soon, we were ushered into a large meeting room, and I met Jeff Lacker in person for the first time. The room was not particularly grand as I might have expected of typical Fed buildings, but it did have tall ceilings and dark-paneled walls. I don't recall seeing any windows. The enclosed nature of the room made it seem perfect for confidential meetings — an impression that added to the somberness of our gathering.

Not that Jeff Lacker himself was somber. He was a pleasant-looking, one might even say handsome, middle-aged gentleman and spoke in the same easy manner as Kevin Warsh. *Do they train them to be like this at the Fed?* I wondered.

The government had seven people at the meeting: Jeff; Grace Dailey from the OCC; Lisa White and Jennifer Burns from the Fed; Mack Alstrom and Sally Green, also from the Fed; and Debra Bailey, who, I gathered, was a senior officer from the D.C Fed office. Debra and I were the only African-Americans in the room. Astonishingly, she would be the only black person I would encounter in any senior government position during my entire time as chairman. She was a very senior official at the Fed, reporting directly to Chairman Bernanke. When we first met, however, she was just another government person on the other side of the table. Grace, Lisa, and Jennifer would become close colleagues of mine over the course of the year, but at this point, they too were just regulators on the other team, and they were about to deliver a painful message.

Jeff, Sally, and Mack sat side-by-side at the huge table. Debra, Lisa, Grace, and Jennifer sat in chairs, arranged closely behind them. The four of us from Bank of America sat across from them. Chad was on the phone. Jeff, who was sitting directly across from me, introduced his team, and then picked up an intimidating looking stack of documents and passed them around. Each document was about one and a half inches thick.

I cannot recount in detail the content of the discussion, or describe the documents we reviewed with the government team, because it is against the law to do so. However, I can say that my colleagues and I listened in a state of shock as Jeff led us through each document. We glanced nervously at each other as if to say, "Are you hearing what I am hearing?"

One of the first things we learned was that the amount of capital we would be required to raise as a result of the recently completed Stress Tests was much more than the bank had anticipated or had planned for. Instituted by Secretary Geithner, the Stress Tests were a process under which every major bank's portfolio would be subjected to a "stress analysis" to determine how the bank would fare in a severe economic turndown. Banks found to be "under-capitalized" would be required to raise capital by issuing more stock, selling assets, increasing earnings, or by various combinations of these and other methods. The results of these tests would be made public, so everyone would know which banks were strong and which were not.

Finally, Jeff looked at me. "You know, Dr. Massey, we're going to be looking to you and your colleagues to make sure your board accomplishes all of the things in this document, and by the deadline noted."

Still looking at me and speaking pleasantly but firmly, he continued: "And when you announce the results of your Stress Test next Thursday, the eyes of the financial community are going to be on you."

As he said this, I asked myself, "Why me?" I hoped that my expression did not betray my worry.

The first time I remember having such severe doubts about my capabilities was in my freshman year at Morehouse College. I arrived at the college in late August of 1954 as a sixteen-year-old, fresh out of the tenth grade in Hattiesburg. I was excited but also anxious and somewhat scared. I wore cream-colored shoes and a shirt my mother had remade from a larger size, and I had my Bible and my alto saxophone with me. Two days after I arrived, I phoned my mother, calling collect from the one payphone in Graves Hall dormitory, my new home. Crying down the phone, I told her I wanted to come home. I was not prepared for this; I would not be able to keep up, I told her. My classmates were from big cities like New York, Chicago, New Orleans, and Dallas, and had attended much better schools. William Churchill, another freshman, had even gone to Andover Academy, a place I had only read about in novels. They were talking about courses they would take and fields they would major in: philosophy, economics, calculus, physics, psychology — subjects I had hardly even heard of.

"How can I compete? I should come home now," I sobbed to my mother.

All she said was, "You'll be all right, son. Just remember, Morehouse would not have given you a Ford Foundation scholarship if they did not believe you could succeed there."

I stayed, of course, but I was still dispirited and depressed afterward.

Three days after that phone call to my mother, the results of the placement examination that all freshmen had to take was posted on the front door of the dormitory. It was a list with the ranking of each of us by name and in order of rank from 1 to about 120, 1 being the highest ranking: Number one, Philip Thompson; number two, William Churchill; number three, Boake Plessy; number four, Frank Green; number five, Walter Massey.

I could not believe it. I was so stunned I almost cried. *Maybe I really am smart*, I thought for the first time. The placement results, and that thought, changed my life. I became more confident in myself and plunged eagerly into classes when school began. *I can do this*, I thought.

I can do this, I thought again as my colleagues and I walked out of the room, where less than two hours earlier, we had taken our seats across from Jeff Lacker and his team of regulators at a mirror-shine mahogany conference table. *I have to do this,* I told myself.

The Fed had given us marching orders that none of us — in fact, no one on the board —had seen coming. We were astounded. We didn't quite know what to do. I'd been chairman for only two days. I didn't have an office. I didn't have a secretary. I had nothing. At this point, I was chairman in name only. Moreover, so much of what was said in the meeting was confidential. When the Fed gives you instructions, it essentially tells you, "you've got to do this, but you have to keep it in-house. It is not for the public." You don't want to talk about it, anyway, because, if the investing community knows the bank is under a mandate of any kind, they will think that the bank is even worse off than it actually was.

There and then, it struck me that this was not going to be the kind of chairmanship I envisioned. I was not going to be the caretaker of the status quo. At the news of my being named chairman of the Bank, the financial community predicted that I would not rock the boat because I was not a finance man, not a banker. For my part, I thought my mandate was to keep a steady hand on the tiller. It was, I believed, to make sure the board worked. *That* I could do. I had chaired boards and organizations, and I learned that I have some talent or skills for chairing. I allow people to talk; I'm good at letting things happen on their own; I'm very good at reaching conclusions. Meetings don't ramble on and on when I'm chairing them. At some point, you have to start bringing things to a conclusion so that the board feels that they accomplished something; that they'd put in a good day's work.

But *this!*

In just three days I had gone on this unimaginable journey, from not even considering the possibility of being chairman of the board of Bank of America, to the euphoria of being named chairman, to being summoned by the Fed and told that I was being held accountable for meeting its requirements to keep the bank from getting into deep trouble. Obviously, the Fed saw in me what I didn't, and they felt comfortable with my leadership. If they were not comfortable, they would have sent a signal to the bank board indicating they could not work with me as chairman. But they hadn't.

Why was the Fed comfortable with *a physicist* as chairman of the board of Bank of America during the worst financial crisis and economic slump since the Great Depression?

Chapter Eight
HOW DID WE GET HERE?

B efore I could give that particular question much thought, a more insistent one surfaced: How did Bank of America get here, to this place of castigation? How did this bank, which, just a few months earlier, enjoyed high praise from the finance, banking, and regulatory world in its audacious leap to national prominence, become the object of the Fed's disapproving eye?

I began to feel that in order to move forward effectively with my new mandate, I needed to re-examine actions the bank had or had not taken, with the blessing of the board, that led to this fall from grace. I also felt I needed to do the same with my own feelings, whether or not I had expressed them, about the positions we took as the collective board.

In some ways, what brought us to where we were was pretty straightforward. We were caught up in the unfolding financial crisis, along with all the other banks. However, our situation was also unique. No other bank was subject to this level of regulatory scrutiny. Certainly, no other had to make board changes, or select a new chairman, as we did.

Of course, the subprime mortgage crash was the immediate trigger for the crisis as a whole. Why didn't we see it coming? I am sure everyone has asked himself or herself that question.

Late in 2007, the mood in financial markets was quite upbeat. At that time, our board and management thought that things seemed to be going exceedingly well. So well, in fact, that it made us feel uneasy. Soon, this uneasiness began to chip away at our high spirits, eventually commandeering the conversation at board meetings and dinners. The same questions, the same assertions, came up over and over again.

"What might go wrong?"

"Things can't keep going this well."

"That's true. There are always cycles."

Many of the veteran bankers and directors recalled the commercial real estate bust of the 1970s, and almost everyone remembered the dot-com bust of the late 1990s and early 2000s. And then there were the near-meltdowns in Asia, Mexico, and Russia. We tried hard to imagine what could trigger a new crisis so that we could be prepared for it.

"Airplane leasing? Mobile home financing? We're exiting those businesses anyway, so we're not really exposed in those markets."

"And we're monitoring our credit card operations very closely."

"What's left that we should worry about?"

"Home mortgages?"

"No. That portfolio is very sound."

True enough, there was little reason to be concerned about residential mortgages at that time. Our losses there had been exceedingly small for years. As bankers say, defaults had been "de minimus," and we had little direct exposure in the subprime mortgage market. We had also reduced our international exposure relative to the size of the bank. Moreover, the bank's huge depositor base buttressed it against the fluctuations of short-term borrowing, unlike the large investment banks that lack deposits and often resort to short-term borrowings.

By the mid-2000s, the general view, which I shared, was that problems in the mortgage market were largely confined to subprime loans, and the risk of a broad meltdown in mortgages was extremely small. There would be no significant spillover from troubles in the subprime market to the rest of the economy or financial system. Even Ben Bernanke, who succeeded Alan Greenspan as Fed chair in 2006, was initially of this mindset.

This widespread reasoning relied upon several observations.

First, it was thought that real estate owners with mortgages wouldn't default in large numbers. If there were defaults, they would not all occur at the same time, and certainly not across the entire country. The thinking also was that housing prices would not plummet everywhere. Indeed, it would be a huge anomaly — and therefore highly improbable — for the entire mortgage system to collapse.

Second, complex securitizations — whereby banks repackage debts such as mortgages and sell the packages to investors — didn't seem to be a threat. Rather, they were viewed as a safeguard. By turning credit and debt into gigantic pools that could be bought and sold as different kinds of securities, the banks assumed that they were spreading the risk over a broad and diverse spectrum of investors and institutions. The whole system, therefore, seemed unlikely to default. Even if defaults occurred, it was unlikely they would do so all at once, throughout the entire system, causing it to crash.

The only caution I recall hearing about these complex securitizations came from our then Chief Financial Officer, Al di Molina. At a meeting of the Asset Quality Committee, Al said he felt the bank was in pretty good shape because we had very little direct exposure to the subprime market. However, he was concerned about the financial markets as a whole because no one really knew where all the mortgage-backed securities and credit default swaps ended up after being sold, repackaged, resold, and resold yet again. Who were the final owners? What was their credit quality? These turned out to be prescient questions.

Third, the risk was thought to be appropriately hedged through credit default swaps, for example, to other financial institutions or private investors, or insured through "monoline" insurance companies that only offer coverage for one specific kind of risk, such as real estate mortgages.

Finally, the rating agencies reinforced the sense of confidence hovering over us. They, after all, were highly reputed for establishing and comparing risk under the most trustworthy, competent, and rigid conditions. At the very least, the markets would generally honor their ratings, and the financial sector respected and interpreted their rankings in the same way.

As we now realize, all of these assumptions proved to be at least partly wrong. But the fragility of the country's widespread confidence still wasn't obvious, even into the middle of 2008.

No one, at least no one on our board or management, foresaw at that time that in less than a year, Bank of America would feel the sting of those incorrect assumptions, or that the eagle glare of regulators, lawmakers, and state officials, would be on us. Certainly, I never foresaw myself as being a central focus for that glare.

CHAPTER NINE

THE "GOOD" NEWS
THAT WASN'T

The bank's acquisitions of Countrywide Financial Corp. and Merrill Lynch exacerbated the effects of the financial crisis on its standing. Each acquisition came about under distinct circumstances. Countrywide's was different because it was so much smaller than Merrill's. Sometimes, in memories of the crises, the two tend to be conflated because of their timing, importance, and eventual bad publicity.

I did not chair any board committees when the bank acquired these entities. I participated actively in board discussions and decisions, but I wasn't a leader in any real sense. I didn't learn that I actually had significant influence until my term as Chairman was almost over. It was when I was having a drink with Anne Finucane, one of the bank's senior officers, that I realized the influence I'd asserted.

Anne said, "Walter, do you know that even before you became chairman when we were preparing for board meetings, we would always say to ourselves, 'What will Walter ask?'"

"You did?" I was genuinely surprised.

"Yes, we did. You always asked such penetrating questions. We knew we had to be prepared."

All I could say was, "Wow! I didn't know that. I'm flattered."

The Countrywide saga began in 2007 when Bank of America provided it with two billion dollars in financing in return for a sixteen-percent stake in the company. At the time, Countrywide was America's number one home loan lender, but it was reeling from a credit crunch, the housing downturn, turmoil in the subprime loan market, and a sharp rise in the number of mortgage holders whose loans were delinquent or in default. As it struggled into the beginning of 2008, Bank of America cemented a deal to buy Countrywide for four billion dollars, in an all-stock transaction.

We thought that buying Countrywide would allow Bank of America to acquire a very large number of retail outlets and business practice with vast experience in servicing reasonably priced mortgages. We also expected Bank of America to improve Countrywide's operations, because Bank of America planned to implement higher standards of mortgage origination and customer service.

The federal government was also eager for us to buy Countrywide, as it saw this as a means of saving, or at least able to stabilize their business. The concern at that time was not about shady or criminal practices. Rather, it was a fear of Countrywide becoming the next big casualty of the crisis.

Before the market collapsed in 2008, the Countrywide acquisition seemed quite manageable. Ken described the transaction in immensely positive terms in the bank's January 11 news release. And indeed, that this was a "positive" transaction that appeared to be the case at the time. But Ken also made it clear that the bank was not oblivious to the problems roiling housing and mortgage markets. He assured the public that these problems had been taken into account in considering the Countrywide purchase.

"We are aware of the issues within the housing and mortgage industries," he asserted in the bank's news release. "The transaction reflects those challenges. Mortgages will continue to be an important relationship product, and we now will have an opportunity to better serve our customers and to enhance future profitability."

I recall feeling very good about the Countrywide purchase and about being on the Bank of America board in general. We were playing an important, significant role in stabilizing the nation's financial systems, and I was immensely proud that we were able to do so and that I was a part of it. At times, Ken used the term "flight to quality" to indicate how ardently we were being sought after as a partner on many fronts — by the government, other financial institutions, and even by customers. I felt we were in a really sound place.

Unfortunately, no one anticipated that Countrywide's portfolio would deteriorate as drastically as it did. Neither did we expect that charges of fraud and deception in mortgage originations would be leveled against its executives, including its reputedly perennially-tanned co-founder and CEO, Angelo Mozilo, who was also charged with insider trading and securities fraud. All of this would come out later. There also was no indication at all at the time of the purchase that Countrywide executives were involved in the kinds of activities that, though not illegal, were certainly questionable, and far below the standards to which Bank of America adhered.

In the fall of 2008, Bank of America was still regarded as one of the soundest and healthiest banks in the country. Then we bought Merrill. The dire condition of the country's financial industry when we made the purchase is well documented in published accounts. At the time, however, not as much was being written specifically about Merrill's vulnerability.

But the fear of contagion was in the air. Financial experts worried most about investment banks, which relied on short-term borrowing to finance their operations. They had far fewer concerns at that time about large, diversified commercial and consumer banks like Wells Fargo, J.P. Morgan, and Bank of America, all of which had access to long-term deposits, Federal Reserve loans, and FDIC insurance. Citibank, though, was rumored to have deep problems.

The memoirs of Henry M. Paulson (*On the Brink: Inside the Race to Stop the Collapse of the Global Financial System*), and Timothy F. Geithner (*Stress Test: Reflections on Financial Crises*), describe that wild weekend in a way that is consistent with my own recollections.

Bank of America's management received various entreaties from government and Federal Reserve officials. One was a request to acquire all or parts of Lehman Brothers, which was facing bankruptcy. On September 12th, day one of the weekend from hell, the bank rejected the request. Ken explained why in an interview with *Fortune* magazine. Lehman held eighty-five billion dollars in toxic commercial and residential real estate loans, and he estimated that ten billion of that was underwater.

Fortune wrote, "He calculated that the value of Lehman's good assets — its investment bank and asset-management arm — wasn't nearly enough to compensate for the potential $10 billion-plus loss on the mortgage assets. He wanted the government to take $65 billion to $70 billion of the most dangerous securities on its books. Over the phone on Friday evening, Lewis told Treasury Secretary Hank Paulson he couldn't buy Lehman without government assistance. When Paulson said he couldn't help, Lewis walked."

Barclays, Britain's third-largest bank, had shown interest in acquiring Lehman, and hopes were high that it would save the day. But it, too, decided not to move forward. There is speculation that, like Bank of America, it had sought assistance from its own regulators in vain.

Ken discussed the bank's decision with the board at our meeting on Sunday, September 14. The next day, Lehman declared bankruptcy.

It was a spectacular moment in the history of banking. It signaled that the subprime mortgage crisis that began in 2007 had not remained confined to the housing sector, as many, including the Fed, had predicted it would. Instead, it had morphed into a full-blown tsunami that ravaged the financial industry.

There's still substantial debate as to whether or not the government should have rescued Lehman. Many believed that it was a mistake not to. Had Lehman been saved as Bear Stearns had been, they argued, the entire crisis might have been averted. Not everyone agrees with this.

Meanwhile, Merrill CEO John Thain had made up his mind. He was determined to speak to Ken. On Saturday, September 13, he phoned Ken at his home in Charlotte with an offer to sell part of Merrill to Bank of America. Ken counter-offered to buy the whole firm.

On Sunday afternoon, in a special teleconference meeting, Ken and the senior management team presented the conditions of a potential transaction with Merrill to the board. This did not come as a complete surprise to me nor, I suspect, to most of the board. A combination of the two companies was not a new idea. In fact, a possible merger with Merrill had been seriously discussed at board meetings several times over the past few years, and several analyses of what a combined company would look like had been considered. Ken had even approached former Merrill CEO Stan O'Neal, earlier about a deal, but at that time, negotiations did not work out. He said O'Neal showed little interest, except under conditions Ken considered unacceptable.

This is really big. Historic, in fact. I couldn't help thinking this as Ken, and his team discussed the likelihood of a Merrill Lynch acquisition. The Merrill Lynch brand arguably was as recognized and respected as Bank of America's.

My thoughts persisted. *This deal will be more important than the BankAmerica-NationsBank deal, and here I am, sitting right in the middle as it's being made!*

My skin tingled at the enormity of it.

Merrill had much to offer the bank, but a primary attraction was its brokerage network of more than sixteen thousand wealth managers and advisors. Sometimes referred to as the "thundering herd," these people were already on the ground, dealing directly with clients. The "thundering herd" would complement Bank of America's existing retail services, including the high-end market it was serving through U.S. Trust. We also determined that Merrill's global investment banking capacity would allow Bank of America to do a better job of serving its growing base of global corporate clients.

All in all, a tremendously advantageous deal.

I was persuaded to support the acquisition primarily because of these considerable strategic benefits. Our board, over the years, had discussed the possibility of building up our presence in investment banking. I thought Merrill would be a good fit. We had, in fact, made an earlier attempt to build up our in-house investment banking by hiring experienced and expensive talent from other firms and allocating more capital to investment banking. But this tactic reaped less than spectacular results. It just didn't work out for us. At one point, Ken was quoted in the press as saying, "I've had about as much fun as I can stand in investment banking."

Another very persuasive argument for going through with the deal at this time was that we thought, reasonably, that Merrill's collapse would likely devastate the entire global financial markets, and would badly damage us along with all the other major financial institutions out there. By acquiring Merrill, the reasoning went, not only would Bank of America own a premier investment bank that fit our projected needs, but also the acquisition would help to stabilize the financial markets when they opened on Monday, September 15.

In short, it would be a win-win — a win for the bank, and a win for the country. We still were seen as one of the strongest and soundest banks in the United States.

"Bank of America! The White Knight to the rescue!" That's how we will be seen, I thought gleefully, feeling even more proud of the bank.

Shirley was curious about the board call. "What was that all about? You don't normally have board meetings on Sunday afternoons. Is something wrong?" she asked after I got off the phone.

I told her I couldn't talk about it then, but nothing was wrong. "In fact, I think it's going to be great," I said. "We'll watch for the news tomorrow."

There was no instant Internet news in those days. Shirley wasn't going to press me. She was content to wait.

I waited anxiously for the deal to be announced that Monday, so Shirley would hear the good news, and I could talk with her about it.

I awoke early and eagerly went to the back door to pick up the papers. I couldn't foresee that eight months from then; I would dread going to the back door to read yet another article by Dan Fitzpatrick in *The Wall Street Journal*. These were the good times. I expected headlines like, "Bank of America acquires Merrill Lynch in historic deal; Markets applaud!"

Shirley pounced as soon as I opened *The Wall Street Journal*. "Well, what does it say? What's the good news?"

"Wait, let me see," I said as I scanned the paper for the "good news."

There was none.

The markets made noise all right, but there was more jeering than applause.

The decision to acquire Merrill was not greeted well. It was immediately controversial. Wall Street asked tough questions about the timing and the cost, and whether the deal was a good strategic fit. The market collapsed even further. There were complaints that we had paid too much, that the potential synergies would be very difficult to achieve, and that providing stability and strength to the thundering herd would destabilize Bank of America.

The collapse of Lehman only deepened concerns about our purchase of Merrill. So, instead of stabilizing after the Merrill purchase, the financial markets became even more uncertain and volatile. Bank stocks declined to such a point that the government decided to intervene further.

In my heart, I knew there would be fallout at Bank of America. Only I had no idea what or how severe it would be.

CHAPTER TEN

THE FALLOUT

On October 13th, 2008, Treasury Secretary Paulson called a meeting in Washington to "offer" the heads of the major investment and commercial banks federal funds to build their capital bases. It was viewed as "an offer the banks could not refuse."

In addition to fifteen billion dollars for Bank of America, ten billion was offered to Merrill Lynch, which was still independent because the merger had yet to close. This was the beginning of the very controversial Troubled Asset Relief Program, which would soon be known as the "bailout." President George W. Bush had signed TARP into law on October 3rd, 2008, authorizing the federal government to buy troubled loans from banks in order to help stabilize the economy.

Ken, and other CEOs, initially resisted the government's offer.

"We don't need the injection of cash. If we took it, we would look even weaker," they argued.

But it truly was an offer that could not be refused. The government felt strongly that the infusion of resources was absolutely necessary to prevent deterioration of the financial system. So, along with all the other banks, we accepted the funds.

It turned out to be a good thing.

Our decision to go through with the deal was not solely because of pressure from Secretary Paulson, though, as the press, members of Congress, and the New York attorney later claimed. Yes, there was pressure from Secretary Paulson to keep us from invoking the MAC. He even threatened to fire the entire board and senior management if we proceeded. We took his frustration and his arguments against invoking the MAC seriously, but we were not really concerned about his "firing" the board. The Treasury had no authority to do such a thing. Even if they had tried, it would have deepened the crisis already roiling the country.

"Who does Hank Paulson think he is? He can't fire us! The shareholders elected us," a longtime board member who knew Paulson fumed during one of our discussions.

That pretty much captured the board's mood. Still, I believe we all appreciated the pressure the Secretary was under and the fact that he and his colleagues were trying to stabilize the financial system by whatever means they could. His — and the Fed's — argument that aborting the Merrill deal would cause havoc in the markets and that Bank of America would suffer along with everyone else, did have some validity. It was persuasive.

So, Paulson was sending a very clear message of how critically the Fed and Treasury viewed the Merrill matter. He and his colleagues at the Fed made it clear that Bank of America could not count on any further government support if the MAC was invoked. Moreover, there was concern that asserting the MAC might not even be successful.

In proceeding with the Merrill deal, we received ample assurance of federal support. The Federal Reserve worked diligently with the Treasury, other regulators, and Bank of America to put in place a package that would help shore up the combined company's financial position and reduce the risk of market disruption. The package included an additional twenty billion dollars' equity investment from the TARP, and a guarantee of 120 billion dollars to absorb future losses at the newly combined company. We also received assurance and a final commitment from the incoming Obama administration that they would honor the Bush administration's agreements. This was very important.

The Treasury and the Fed requested that our negotiations with them be held in strict confidence. We complied, but it caused us severe problems later.

Suddenly, during the November-December period, when much of the drama surrounding Merrill's acquisition was unfolding, Bank of America took a backseat in my mind as a frightening situation arose in my personal life.

One night, early in November, just shy of a month before shareholders approved the merger with Merrill, I awoke in the middle of the night with terrible pains in my lower abdomen. Shirley heard me moaning. She sat up and looked at me, her eyes wide with worry.

"What's the matter, Walter? Walter! What's the matter! Are you okay?"

"I don't know. I have a pain on my left side," I said weakly.

I got out of bed to go to the bathroom. The pain was so bad I could hardly walk.

"We should go to the emergency room. It may be something serious." Shirley seemed calm, but her voice conveyed her concern.

"No. Let's just wait until tomorrow and see how I feel."

It was no better in the morning.

"We're going to the emergency room right now," Shirley said.

I didn't protest.

I was a former faculty member, senior administrator, and current trustee of the University of Chicago, so I was seen almost immediately at the University's Medical Center. I was still feeling that I was going to be okay.

"It can't be that bad," I told myself.

It was.

An X-ray showed a large growth in my lower colon. The doctor was blunt.

"It's infected, Walter, and may burst at any time. I assure you, you don't want to experience the consequences of that. You need to be admitted immediately. We have to operate right away."

I was alarmed and showed it. Shirley was calm, outwardly at least.

"Well, then. Let's get you admitted, Walter," she said.

The operation successfully removed the growth, but I had to spend the next eleven days in the hospital. Shirley had a cot placed in my room and slept there almost every night.

During this time, I was viewing the issues at the bank, almost as if I were simply a member of the public instead of a member of the board. I was prohibited from flying for more than a month, so I participated in board meetings by phone.

I was released two days after Thanksgiving. When I got home, I was greeted with a wonderful meal that our neighbor, Carol Hartzmark, had prepared. It was my first real meal in almost two weeks. I was fed intravenously for most of the time I was in the hospital. In the last two days of my stay, I feasted on mushy hospital food. Meanwhile, our co-op neighbors had been sending Shirley food the entire time I was hospitalized. It was well known throughout the building that I did all the cooking in our home.

Although I felt less than fully recovered, I was on top of the world during my convalescence. Just before I went into the hospital, I was elected to the board of the United States Tennis Association, which was a dream come true for a tennis fanatic like me. Not only would I be immersed in the national tennis scene and get to meet tennis greats, but Shirley and I would also be invited to attend every session of the two-week U.S. Open and watch from the president's suite. In addition, we'd get to go to Davis and Fed Cup matches throughout the world.

"What could be better than this?" I asked myself.

Then came the public announcement of Merrill's 2008 fourth-quarter losses, and the Federal Reserve's infusion of cash on January 16th, 2009, along with guarantees to help the bank absorb any additional "unusually large losses."

Reality crept back in.

But I was still just one of nineteen directors. With all of the problems we had with Merrill and the headaches it cost us, its acquisition would turn out to be a very positive and profitable move for the bank. At the time, however, little did I know that the controversy surrounding the acquisition had set the stage for the contentious shareholder meeting of April 29th, 2009, and for my being named chairman of the board at the meeting that followed the same day.

Chapter Eleven
LOOKING TO THE PAST FOR LESSONS LEARNED

But why me?

I could not help returning to that question.

Our group was still in the lobby of the Richmond Fed. We sat close to each other around a low coffee table. For a while, no one spoke. It was as though each of us needed time to process the hand we had just been dealt.

My mind reeled. Why *did* the Fed and the other agencies have confidence in me as the best person for the job as chairman? I was a physicist. Could I justify that confidence?

This was not the first time I was called upon in a time of crisis. I was seventy-one years old. For forty of those years, I had held prominent positions in academia and U.S. government institutions and served on the boards for major corporations. Quite often, I had found myself at the heart of pivotal circumstances. Surely, I was adequately prepared for a situation such as this, daunting as it seemed. At least I hoped so.

I tried to think of past experiences that might serve me here. No matter how hard I tried to focus, my mind tugged like a dog on a leash toward 1968. It was the year of the assassinations of presidential candidate Robert "Bobby" F. Kennedy, and civil rights leader Martin Luther King, Jr., the year of riots and burnings around the country, and the year of the Democratic Party's convention in Chicago, which was marred by internal chaos over the party's position on the Vietnam War, as tens of thousands of anti-Vietnam War protesters clashed violently with police outside in the streets.

It was also the year of my traumatic divorce from my first wife, Judy, and later, the year I met Shirley.

I met Judy Whitmore in St. Louis while I was working on my Ph.D. at Washington University. She had studied Spanish in college and was teaching at a local high school. She was an attractive woman, fun to be with, and the first woman with whom I had a serious sexual relationship. I was in love and wanted to get married. She accepted my proposal, and we married in 1964. After I graduated in 1966, we moved to Chicago and took up residence on Drexel Avenue in the Hyde Park neighborhood.

My younger brother, Al, was living in Chicago when Judy and I arrived. He had been there since he left Hattiesburg in 1960. We didn't see each other a lot when I was in graduate school, but we had gone through a very traumatic experience when our mother died in 1963, and we had to bury her in Chicago. It's a story that warrants much more than these few lines, one I intend to tell in future writings.

Al had a small business supplying cleaning services to companies of all kinds and was very engaged in Chicago politics. He knew how the city worked and helped to educate me.

When Judy and I moved from St. Louis to Chicago, I drove our car with a small trailer hooked up to the back. All our household items were stuffed inside. We didn't have very much. As I entered the city, I exited from the Dan Ryan Expressway onto 55th Street, which led directly into Hyde Park. After a few blocks, I was pulled over by Chicago police. Strangely, I was more curious than afraid or anxious, unlike the fear or anxiety black people might feel today when police pull us over. The officer, an older white man, neatly dressed in his uniform, spoke very politely.

"You do know you shouldn't have that trailer on this street, right?"

"No. Why?"

"This is a boulevard — Garfield Boulevard as well as 55th Street. In Chicago, it is illegal to drive trucks or have trailers on boulevards," he said.

"Really? I did not know that," I told him, "and I didn't see any signs that indicated that when I left the Dan Ryan."

He said, "Well, it is illegal. So, what do you want to do about it?"

I was puzzled. "I don't know. What do I need to do?"

"Well, I could give you a ticket, and you would have to pay it or go to court."

"Well ... if I have to, that's OK, I guess."

He looked at me with disgust, it seemed, and wrote the ticket. Two weeks later, as I was driving to pick up Judy from the high school where she had gotten a job as a Spanish teacher, I was pulled over for violating another obscure law having to do with not coming to a full stop before turning into a boulevard. This officer went through the same routine after explaining to me what I had done.

"Well, what are you going to do about it?"

Since I did not know what to do about it, I received another ticket. I now had two traffic violations. A third would cost me my license. I called Al and described what had happened. Laughing loudly, he said, "Walt, don't you know what you are supposed to do about it?"

"No. I have no idea."

"Well, when you show your driver's license, you fold up a five-dollar bill and hand it to the cop with the license. On the north side, it's ten dollars, but five dollars will do on this side of town," he said, still chuckling.

This was my first lesson in how the city really worked.

The 1960s were exciting enough, but our Hyde Park location on the south side of Chicago made our lives even more exhilarating. Hyde Park was home to the University of

Chicago, the Museum of Science and Industry, the world's first nuclear reactor, and the Frederick C. Robie House — a National Historic Landmark that was designed by renowned architect Frank Lloyd Wright in what is considered the first uniquely American architectural style. I had gotten a job as a research scientist at the great Argonne National Laboratory, and my salary, coupled with Judy's, made it possible for us to live in Hyde Park. Except for one year I taught at Morehouse, I had never held a serious, full-time job. Up to that point, I had spent most of my life as a student. Now I had a real job — as a physicist! — which made me wonderfully contented.

Yet, despite all the excitement, the prideful sense of achievement, and the promise of the future that I felt, our marriage did not last and ended in a divorce, which was most painful for me. I sank into a deep depression. I was hardly able to work, hardly able to sleep. Judy moved out, and I stayed in the apartment we had shared. I don't know what I would have done without my good friend, Avon Kirkland, who consoled and counseled me. He got me involved in a local musical theatre group, where I learned to sing and dance in musicals like *Kiss Me Kate*, *Fiorello*, and *Finian's Rainbow*. That really helped to cheer me up.

Although I was no stranger to the stage or to performing before an audience, given my Blue Gardenia experience, I didn't realize I could also sing somewhat decently. My parts were mostly in the "chorus" and minor roles, but I loved learning the dance routines. One of my very favorite roles was in *Kiss Me Kate*, where I was cast as a member of the quartet that performed the song, "Brush Up Your Shakespeare." I still love that song.

Avon, meanwhile, was a very good singer and dancer and always had the leading man roles. Avon and I first met when we were undergraduates, I at Morehouse and he at Clark College next door. We both wound up in graduate school at Washington University, where he was pursuing a Ph.D. in chemistry, while I was pursuing mine in physics. We shared an apartment for three years and became lifelong friends. He is still among my very best friends.

Avon was living in Chicago at the time Judy and I divorced. His support was crucial for me to overcome this traumatic experience and begin a new chapter in my life. That's when he introduced me to Shirley Anne Streeter, the beautiful and charismatic woman who later became my wife.

He called me one night. I'll never forget the date — April 4, 1968, the night Martin Luther King, Jr. would be assassinated.

"Hey, Walt. How are you feeling?" He sounded excited.

"Pretty good. I was just watching TV." I must have sounded dull.

"Man, I just met this girl I really think you ought to meet," Avon gushed.

"Really? I am not sure I want to get involved with anyone right now."

"Well, I think you should. She is gorgeous. She's got these sparking light-green eyes. And when I asked her what she liked, she said 'sex!'"

"That's interesting. Sex?"

"Yes! "Sex" is what she said."

"Well, OK then," I said to Avon, half-jokingly.

Avon was dating a good friend of Shirley's named Bonita Byrd and met Shirley at Bonita's apartment. Later, when I asked Shirley about Avon's account of their meeting, she said, "I had gotten so tired of guys saying to me, 'Well, what do you like?' that I decided to be shocking."

"Well, it didn't work," I laughed.

Shirley invited me to dinner one night at her apartment and introduced me to her six-year-old son, Keith, and his friend Eric. She lived in a very small apartment above a drugstore and lunch counter, right in the center of Hyde Park, on one of the busiest corners. There was one bedroom, a small closet-size room where Keith slept, a living room, and a tiny kitchen. Everything was very neat and organized. She was as beautiful as Avon had described, modestly dressed, as she would say later, "like a Catholic girl who had to go downtown every day to work." She always wore gloves and stockings when she went downtown and didn't look at all like the girl whose favorite avocation was sex.

She was cooking spaghetti when I arrived at her apartment. She was not a very good cook, and it showed, so I changed her plans and cooked the spaghetti dinner myself. The boys were ecstatic. They loved the meal.

That was the start of our relationship. We were married a year and a half later. Shirley has often said that she decided she was going to marry me when she saw how I behaved with her son and his friend. She also says she will always remember she first knew of my existence the night Martin Luther King was assassinated, one day before my birth date, April 5th. Marrying Shirley changed my life in so many ways. In two short years, I went from being a divorced bachelor to a family man with a delightful son, Keith, which I felt gave me a new sense of responsibility and maturity. I was not a particularly shy person before I met Shirley, but I certainly wasn't gregarious. I did not make new friends easily.

One of the things I loved about theoretical physics research was its solitary nature. I discovered physics through my love of mathematics. I took my first physics course in my sophomore year at Morehouse, and I was fascinated. I found physics was a way to apply mathematics to understanding the world around us. Theoretical physics was the best combination of physics and mathematics. True, you work with collaborators and other colleagues during research, but much of the time, you are working alone — just you, pen, and paper — trying to understand some complex mathematical, physical phenomenon. There is a great deal of contemplation and withdrawal from the world around you. There is a solitude and total absorption that is as close to a meditative state as I have ever achieved.

Shirley was outgoing and friendly, even with strangers. And she was exceptionally beautiful. She attracted attention all the time. On airplanes, in restaurants, the grocery checkout line, at the cleaners, even simply walking down the street, strangers, especially women, would come up to her and make admiring comments.

"Oh, you have the most beautiful eyes," they would say.

And, "I could see your eyes from across the room; they are so bright and sparkling."

And, "I hope you don't mind, but I just had to come over and say you are so pretty. And those eyes!"

And so on.

Shirley had learned to take all these comments graciously. Typically, she would strike up a conversation with her admirers. "You should have seen my mother's eyes. I got mine from her," she would say. Or, "Thank you so much. Where are you from? Is that your daughter? My, she is pretty." Being with her made me a center of attention and, strangely — maybe it wasn't so strange — gave me more confidence in dealing with strangers and making new friends. We were, and still are, a very popular couple. As an old song goes, "We walk into a room, a party, or ball, 'come sit over here,' somebody will call."

Eddie Higgins, the very well-known, popular jazz pianist, lived near us on Cape Cod in the summers, and we became friends. Whenever we walked into a club where he was playing, the moment he saw Shirley, he would stop whatever he and his group were playing and launch into *The Most Beautiful Girl in The World*. The entire club would turn to stare at her. Eddie passed away in 2009.

Without Shirley, I never would have been as successful as I have been in all the positions I had after physics research, positions that required extraordinary people skills, which Shirley had an abundance of, and shared with me.

Chapter Twelve
1968: EVEN MORE INSTRUCTIVE

The year 1968 was also when I began as an assistant professor of physics at the University of Illinois at Urbana-Champaign, my first faculty job. Just as I was hit in the face with the Fed's directives right after my election as chairman, so, too, on my very first night at Urbana — September 9th — I was slammed with the racial, political, and social issues roiling the campus.

The telephone rang, literally in the middle of the night.

"Professor Massey?" The caller spoke as soon as I picked up.

"Who?" I was thirty years old and nobody had ever addressed me as 'Professor.' It dawned on me almost immediately that I was the 'professor' in question. I recovered quickly.

"Oh! Yes. This is Professor Massey."

"Professor Massey, this is David Addison. They've just arrested 250 black students at a sit-in at the Illini Union, and we're trying to get faculty members to come down to help get them out." The Illini Union was the student center.

David was president of the newly established Black Students Association. It took a while to get all the details from him. I didn't know my way around Champaign yet, and by the time I arrived at the jail, the situation seemed to be under control. Bail was being arranged. I was not called on to do anything more that morning. But the incident marked the beginning of a year and a half of deep, sometimes frustrating, involvement in the racial, political, and social issues of the time, which were reflected on many college campuses.

David got me engaged as the Black Students Association's faculty adviser, and I also helped to form the Black Faculty and Staff Association and became its first chairman. We were constantly called upon to mediate between students and the administration. I felt close to burning out during many of these months. I wanted to be involved with students, with the issues of the day, but I didn't expect to be hit in the face so quickly.

I had left my job as a research scientist at Argonne National Laboratory because I wanted to teach and counsel students, and perhaps create special science programs for minority students. I accepted an offer to join the faculty at Urbana in the summer of 1968 because the physics department was one of the very best in the world in my field of research, Condensed Matter Theory. The faculty included two-time Nobel Prize winner John Bardeen, and Gordon Baym and Leo Kadanoff, two young, brilliant theorists. Gordon and Leo were instrumental in convincing me to accept the offer from the University.

As much as I wanted to be engaged with social issues, I also very much wanted to develop my physics skills by working with and learning from these and other established figures. Instead, I found myself not really devoting as much time to my physics as I wanted or needed. I also didn't feel that I was making a real difference on the racial and social fronts. I was constantly putting out brush fires just to hold things together. I saw no strategy, no long-range goals where I would make a substantial strategic difference.

Because of my engagement in so many activities around campus, I did get to know and work closely with the Chancellor, Jack Peltason, who would play a pivotal role in my career much later on.

'Burn out' became a common occurrence among young, black faculty. I was one of fewer than ten black "tenure track" faculty among about a thousand faculty members at Urbana.

Back then, it was common for young, black faculty members to be called upon to be intensely involved in any and all racial issues on campus. This was all very good until it came time for tenure decisions, and black faculty were often denied tenure because they had not devoted enough time to their research. Suddenly all the engagement with students didn't really matter.

I began to feel that my situation was untenable. Then help came to me early in the fall of 1969, in the form of a letter from my friend, Leo Kadanoff, the world-renowned theoretical physicist who had recruited me to Urbana. Leo had become my mentor and closest colleague at Urbana, but he moved to Brown University in 1969, shortly after I joined the faculty.

The letter stated he really liked Brown and wanted to talk to me about coming there.

We spoke on the phone, and he invited me to visit.

He said, "Walter, here you will have a lot more freedom to do physics and work on issues that interest you. They're a lot more flexible here. I have a joint appointment in Physics and Urban Studies, and I can do research in both areas. I feel like I am contributing something to the social issues of the times without giving up physics."

This sounded very attractive, but it would mean leaving Urbana after only a year and a half, and that bothered me. Was I bailing out? Would Brown really be better?

After visiting Brown and meeting some of the key people there, I decided to take the plunge. Shirley and I got married in October 1969, and we headed off to Brown the following January.

I went to Brown in mid-semester as a tenured associate professor of physics, the first African-American in that role. If eyes were on me then, I can only imagine how many more were on me and how much more scrutinous they were when I became Dean of the College five years later.

I was a bachelor when I first visited Brown in the early fall of 1969. So, when I showed up married and with a son, it was quite a surprise to many, especially to my department chairman.

I immediately wanted to renegotiate the salary I had accepted, which would have been fine for a single person, but not for a family of three. As Leo had noted, Brown was a very flexible place, and indeed, I did get a raise — timely too, because fairly soon, our younger son, Eric, was born, and we now had two kids and two cats. Later on, we added two dogs.

At Urbana, I had developed an interest in pre-college science education because I saw up close how many students from the inner cities struggled to keep up with college physics. Science education in high school was clearly a problem. I saw science education as a way for me to contribute something substantive and meaningful to the civil rights movement.

"I'm a scientist. Can't I invest the resources at Brown to do something about the problem?" I thought. "I must be able to figure out a way to teach science in high school so that when students get to college, they'll be able to do the courses."

I developed a project called ICTOS, an acronym for Inner City Teachers of Science, whose aim was to attract and educate students early in their college careers to teach science in inner-city schools. Herman Eschenbacher, a professor of education at Brown, became my main partner in ICTOS. We strategized, applied to the National Science Foundation for a major grant, and — lo and behold — we got it. We'd said ICTOS would be multidisciplinary, so we had to find chemists, biologists, and engineers to participate. That got me working with faculty all over the campus.

This was my first taste of administrative leadership, and I'm sure it led to my becoming better known on campus and seeming capable of larger duties. I was also learning that I had a knack for getting people from different backgrounds and disciplines to work together on major projects. They accepted me as the organizer and leader and liked me in that role. And I found I enjoyed it. There was a purpose to it. I liked learning that when I saw a situation that called for action, I could look for the strategic path to what's really going to make the difference.

IN THE EYE OF THE STORM

Putting together ICTOS made me so well-known across the campus that I was asked to apply for the position of Dean of the College, a very prestigious position at Brown. I did, and I got the job. This was a really big deal. I now had to worry about how to keep my physics research going, but others had done it, so why couldn't I? It happened that the Dean of the College at Yale, Horace Taft (Yes, of the Taft family of Ohio that sired the twenty-seventh president and tenth chief justice of the United States) was also a physicist, and became a role model for me.

I learned a critical lesson in leadership when the university undertook a budget restructuring. The entire University had to downsize. We were curtailing programs everywhere. As dean of the college, I was given a budget but told I had to reduce the existing one, which meant I had to reduce the staff. I went about it analytically. I studied the existing budget, reviewed the staff, and talked to people to determine which positions we could eliminate. I had to eliminate the position of one woman — I'll call her Laura — who had been with Brown for a very long time. In my mind, I was going to sit down with her, explain how I arrived at my decision, and we would shake hands and talk about her future.

But when we met, and I told her my decision, she started to cry.

"I've worked here for such a long time. I don't know what I would do if you fired me, Walter," she sobbed.

Laura was in her early fifties. It was no secret that her husband, a professor, struggled with alcoholism. Her work on campus was likely an escape from all that.

I was taken aback. I did not know how to deal with these emotions. I tried to comfort her to no avail. I really felt very bad, but in the end, I had no choice but to let her go. The episode made me start to think differently. I began to think more about the human issues in running an organization, not just budgets and strategic planning.

"Walter, you are dealing with people, real-life human beings who have issues and whose lives you're affecting. This is not an abstract exercise," I told myself.

Shirley was very good in helping me to become more aware of these issues. I went home that afternoon, still disturbed, and described to her what had happened,

She said, "Well, what did you expect, Walter? What is she going to do? It's not only losing the job but also the embarrassment of being let go and the loss of a dignified position in the community. And everyone likes her."

All I could do was nod in agreement.

CHAPTER THIRTEEN
MY ONLY OPTION

The recollection of Laura's raw emotion and her plea — "What will I do?" — drew me back to the lobby outside the boardroom of the Richmond Fed.

"Let's make sure we all heard the same thing in there," Tom May was saying. "I took notes. Here's what I heard them say."

Tom proceeded to read from his notes. He had, in fact, taken meticulous notes during our meeting with Jeff Lacker and his team. Much later, as we worked through the issues raised by the Fed, I found that kind of note-taking to be characteristic of him.

When he finished reading, he looked around our tight huddle, intently scanning each face. "Is that what you recall hearing them say? Did I get it right? Did I get everything down?"

"Yes," Frank, Charles, and I agreed in chorus.

Tom had done such a great job keeping notes that we were quickly able to agree on what we had heard and begin to consider our next steps. Tom even faxed me a copy of his notes that evening.

So, within fifty-three hours of taking over as chairman, I was facing perplexing challenges posed by the Fed's mandate, beginning with making major changes in our corporate governance and reconstituting the board. There also was concern that the financial system might face further meltdowns, and we were told that Bank of America needed a massive infusion of capital to survive such a crisis. We might need a change in leadership. Would that mean replacing Ken Lewis as CEO?

Frank Bramble made one of the most consequential suggestions. "We need to get some assistance. We should get hold of Ed Herlihy. He's one of the most prominent lawyers in the financial world," Frank volunteered. "And I have worked with him before on issues like this."

Frank had experienced a similar crisis when he was CEO of Maryland National Bank and knew we needed to engage outside counsel. Edward D. Herlihy was a partner at the law firm Wachtell, Lipton, Rosen, & Katz and had served as counsel for the bank. He became a precious resource in all my work as chairman, both for legal counsel and advice in general.

"This is very bad," Frank said, "but at least we did not get a 'Cease and Desist' order. That is deadly."

I did not know what Frank meant then but later learned that a 'Cease and Desist Order' was the most severe penalty that the Fed could issue. It can call for drastic restrictions, and it is made public, so shareholders, customers, and the general public are aware of it. Our 'Agreement,' on the other hand, was 'strictly confidential,' although that didn't stop leaks from happening.

"First of all, the five of us, Chad included, have to get together because one of the primary things we heard we have to do is change the board," I told them. "That means we'll have to ask some people to leave, so we have to meet as a team."

The comments that ensued seemed to tumble over each other.

"But the board hasn't appointed us to do anything. How are we going to do this? By whose authority are we going to accomplish these things we've been asked to do?"

"We have to act. We have a document from the Fed. We have to take that to the board and have them delegate us to do these things."

"That's tricky. How do you convene a meeting to tell the board what happened, and then ask them to give us the authority to do what the Fed wants us to do? The other board members weren't there, so why should they give us that authority?"

"That's a good point. They have just as much right as any of us. We're just a subset of the board. We just have to hope that after hearing our report, they will agree."

I began to understand why Jeff Lacker did not want me to go to Richmond alone, but to take other members of the board with me. I couldn't imagine having to deliver this news all by myself.

"We can't convene the full board right away, and we have to get started on this work right now," Tom said.

"I'll need staff support, someone I can count on to work closely with me and who also is familiar with the bank," I said. The answer came instantly. "What about Alice?"

Alice Herald was secretary to the board and an assistant general counsel. She would become my all-important confidante.

"We've got to tell Ken," someone pointed out.

The four of us agreed that I would call Ken Lewis and that we would try to get together as soon as possible. We had to move fast because the federal government was about to release the findings of the two-month-long 'Stress Tests' it had conducted to determine how much extra capital the largest U.S. banks needed in order to withstand the most adverse financial conditions and still remain solvent.

Nineteen banks, including Bank of America, underwent the tests, which were known formally as the Supervisory Capital Assessment Program, or SCAP. My first public duty as chairman would be to announce how Bank of America had fared. The results were scheduled to be released to the public in six days on Thursday, May 7th. The financial and political communities were eagerly awaiting them because they would indicate, supposedly, which banks were viewed as well-capitalized and which ones weren't. Our own bank's management, meanwhile, had done an internal assessment, and we knew we'd have to raise a significant amount of new capital.

In our meeting with the Fed, however, Jeff told us that the results showed Bank of America needed to raise nearly thirty-four billion dollars in additional capital. We were visibly shaken. This was much more than the bank's internal assessment had suggested. The difference between the two assessments involved variables such as what could be counted as capital, the riskiness of our loan and credit portfolios, and views of the overall economy. Other major banks had similar disagreements with the Fed.

"Dr. Massey," Jeff had said from across the table, "when the Stress Test results are announced next Thursday, the eyes of the financial community are going to be on you."

The bank's press release about the SCAP test wouldn't simply be my first public statement from the chair. My statement would have to deliver a credible message. I thought again that the government could have called for a new chairman, someone with more banking and financial experience. My only option was to do my best, and my best was grounded in the many valuable lessons I had learned in times past, as much from experiences where I had prevailed as from those where I had not. All offered lessons for me.

Chapter Fourteen
I FELT READY

In 1979, while I was Dean and professor at Brown, I left the university to become the first African-American director of Argonne National Laboratory, a major center of national and international research, especially in nuclear energy. Argonne was the direct descendant of the laboratory where physicist Enrico Fermi initiated the first self-sustained nuclear chain reaction in December 1942, ushering in the nuclear age. Fermi's lab was located under the old bleachers of Stagg Field stadium at the University of Chicago.

Looking back over my life, I've found that a willingness to be open to possibilities quite different from your expectations greatly benefits your professional pursuits. I've learned, too, that people do make a difference in your life. So many of my 'door openings' have come about because I got to know someone who was impressed with me personally.

How, for example, did a theoretical physicist and Dean of the College at Brown, having never directly managed more than fifty or sixty people, become director of one of the nation's historic, most iconic, and strategically important research institutions, Argonne National Laboratory? The answer lies with Hanna Gray.

Hanna is one of the country's most distinguished historians. More pertinent to this memoir, however, is her reputation as a pioneer in breaking through the glass ceiling in higher education administration. Just as I was the first black in many of the positions I held, she was the first woman in numerous roles, including Dean of Arts and Sciences at Northwestern University; provost and subsequently acting president at Yale; and president of the University of Chicago.

I first met Hanna when she was acting president at Yale, and I was Dean of the college at Brown. Shirley and I attended a Yale-Brown football game in New Haven (Brown lost in the last few seconds), and Hanna hosted a reception at the president's house after the game. Somehow, she and I hit it off. But this was a social gathering.

The following year, 1978, Brown awarded an honorary degree to Hanna, who was then President of the University of Chicago. I was her faculty host when she came to receive the degree. I was assigned to accompany her to all of the related events to make sure she had whatever she needed — essentially to see that she was comfortable and at ease with everything. Shirley and I spent quite a bit of time with her, and Hanna and I got to know each other better. She also learned as she said later on numerous occasions, how much I was admired by students, faculty, and other administrators at Brown.

One day in early 1979, I received a call from Hanna. I was in my Dean's office at Brown, which truly was classically elegant, with a wood-burning fireplace, Oriental/Persian/antique wool carpets, the muted scent of oak shelves and cabinets and leather-bound books, and a magnificent view overlooking the main quadrangle. It was as though it was lifted right out of the movies about Ivy League colleges that I had seen as a youngster.

I greeted Hanna. "Hi, Hanna. How are things in Chicago?"

"Things are good here, Walter. And I continue to hear great things about you," she replied."

"Well, I'm glad to hear that. Shirley and I really love it here," I said.

"I am not surprised. When I was there, I could see how much they loved you two," she said, and then she went to the point of her call. "Walter, you may not have heard yet, but we are looking for a new director of Argonne and would like your ideas on what kind of person we should be considering. Would you be willing to speak with Bill Cannon, the vice president, who is responsible for the university's oversight of the lab, to give him your views?"

"Of course, Hanna. Definitely have him give me a call," I said. It was a most flattering request.

"Oh no," she said quickly. "He would like to see you in person if that's OK."

"Sure. I would be happy to meet him."

I learned much later that this was a classic way to size up a possible candidate for a position without directly asking them to consider it. "*We want to hear your views on the kind of person we should be considering.*" I later used the same approach when recruiting people for top positions at other institutions I would lead.

Several weeks after meeting with Bill Cannon, Hanna called and asked me to consider being interviewed for the position of director of Argonne. I was interviewed and subsequently offered the position. As a director, I reported to Hanna, who became one of the most important mentors in my life.

So, a little over ten years after Avon introduced us, Shirley and I moved back to Hyde Park, but not in the same circumstances. I was now the head of one of the most important institutions in the area, and also a professor at the University of Chicago, which came with the Argonne position. Shirley's old friends who grew up with her and watched her navigate life as a working single mother were very happy to see her in such prestigious positions. No one was prouder than her dad, William 'Bill' Streeter. Bill was the first black janitor at the University of Chicago. He spent his entire working career at the University of Chicago Laboratory School in that position. To see his daughter return to the neighborhood like this was a source of great pride to him.

Shirley and I moved into a beautiful, historic, art deco building right on Lake Michigan, with two kids, two cats, and two dogs.

During my tenure at Argonne, I became familiar with the intricacies of managing a large organization and carrying out complex negotiations with the federal government. Up to that point, the largest entity I had ever managed was the dean's office at Brown, where fewer than one hundred people reported to me. I had worked at Argonne as a research scientist from 1966 to 1968 during my doctoral studies and continued working there in the summers when I was at Brown.

When I returned as director in May 1979, I had a staff of 5,200 people, an annual budget of almost $403 million, and two crises staring me in the face: a threat to the lab's government funding, and a crossroads in the development of nuclear energy. Just two months before my arrival, a near catastrophe at the Three Mile Island nuclear plant in Pennsylvania added a sobering factor to discussions of a national nuclear energy policy. Already I could see that running Argonne would present its challenges.

This truly was a circumstance of learning on the job. First, I had to learn about the issues. The University of Chicago operates the lab, but the United States government, through the Department of Energy, owned it and financed it. Its main program was research on the use of nuclear reactors to generate electricity. I didn't really understand how the funding worked. I knew in principle, but I did not know who really called the shots in Washington — who influenced what happened in the lab. I spent a lot of time making sense of those intricacies, traveling back and forth to Washington, and meeting people in the lab.

Next, I had to learn a lot about nuclear power and the politics surrounding the nuclear program at the lab and in Washington. Once I understood that I had to try to formulate a strategy to preserve funding for the lab. There were rumors in Washington that the DOE was considering closing one of its major labs, and Argonne was high on the list. Later, when rumors of bank nationalizations abounded, I was reminded of this period.

I put together different groups in the lab to work on specific areas. One area of work was to develop a strategic plan for a new role in nuclear power research and development at the lab. Argonne's expertise was nuclear energy. We would 'sell' the lab to the government as a first-class resource in nuclear power research, doing what no other lab could, and in a new technology called 'fast breeder reactors.' Our plan was just beginning to take shape when Ronald Reagan came into office and immediately began to slash the funding for our alternative energy research — the solar and environmental programs. We had to lay off six hundred people.

That was a big deal. I only had experience laying off one person, 'Laura,' at Brown. Now I was responsible for terminating the jobs of six hundred people. We had to put together a plan that would allow us to keep the very best people. That's harder than it might sound.

I did not forget the lesson I had learned in Laura's case: you're impacting the lives of human beings, people with real-life issues. Lying off six hundred people wasn't just an abstract operation. We had to be thoughtful. I had a very good leadership team — many were more experienced than me, and some had been through similar situations, just as Frank Bramble had been through similar situations with the Fed. I learned a great deal from the team. We carried out the layoffs in what turned out to be an exemplary manner, even garnering positive feedback from some of the individuals who were affected.

Because of my visibility with Argonne, a host of professional groups and the boards of some of Chicago's largest corporations invited me to join them. Among these were Amoco Oil, which later became part of British Petroleum; First National Bank of Chicago, or First Chicago, which later merged into JPMorgan Chase; Motorola; the Tribune Company; the Chicago Cubs (my favorite board); and the MacArthur Foundation. In accepting these invitations, I began to learn more than I ever expected about the governance of large organizations — corporate, philanthropic, and otherwise. I found that my scientific and administrative background, as well as the people-skills I had learned along the way, proved useful for board work.

No experience was as eerily similar to what I would encounter as chairman of Bank of America as my membership on First Chicago's board of directors. First Chicago was the largest bank in the city and one of the ten largest in the country. When I joined the board in 1984, I was still learning about serving on corporate boards, and I knew almost nothing about banking. As with all of the boards I joined, I set out to learn as much as I could. I read all about it, sought out mentors, and spent time with senior executives, some of whom became my tutors. William McDonough, who subsequently became president of the Federal Reserve Bank of New York, tutored me on asset and liability control and many other aspects of the banking industry.

My most valuable mentor at both First Chicago and Amoco was John Bryan, then chief executive of the Sara Lee Corporation and, as it happened, a fellow Mississippian. I didn't have a financial background, but because of my mathematical training, I was a quick study once I'd learned the language of finance and accounting. John Bryan remained a close friend and mentor until he died in the spring of 2019.

As it happened, I joined the First Chicago board at a particularly auspicious time for banking in Chicago. The same year, the city's other major bank, Continental Illinois National Bank and Trust Company — headquartered just a few blocks from First Chicago — became the largest bank to ever fail in the United States, and would remain so until Washington Mutual, the country's largest savings and loan bank, collapsed in 2008.

At the time of its debacle, which was attributed to the acquisition of bad oil and gas loans from Oklahoma City's Penn Square Bank, Continental Illinois was the seventh-largest bank in the country and the largest in the Midwest, with $307 billion in assets. Naturally, its failure caused great consternation at First Chicago. Although we were not invested in the activities that affected Continental, the mere fact that a bank about the size of First Chicago could actually fail and wipe out shareholder's investments was sobering. We increased our internal due diligence, and the federal regulatory agencies increased external diligence.

Then, in 1985, we had our own crisis. We suffered major losses after investing $14.6 million to acquire a 44.5 percent stake in Banco Denasa de Investimento S.A., a small, financially unsound investment bank in Brazil. It turned out that the president of Denasa, who also was its majority shareholder, falsely represented the bank's value in the negotiations with First Chicago and did not disclose that Brazil's Central Bank was looking into irregularities in the bank's financial statements. The investment proved to be a disaster for us at First Chicago and led to major losses. The Office of the Comptroller of the Currency, First Chicago's primary regulator, was so perturbed about the bank's condition that its deputy director traveled to Chicago to meet directly with the bank's board of directors. He expressed the agency's concerns in very strong language and handed us a set of marching orders.

"We're requiring you to commit to certain actions to stem the persistent loan losses," he announced in a tone that permitted no argument. "If the losses persist, we may require you to make major changes in the bank's management. I remind you that as directors, you are responsible for overseeing the management of the bank."

We were on the top floor of the iconic First National Bank of Chicago building in the very heart of the city's business district. The building sweeps sixty floors upward, curving from a 200-foot wide base at street level to 95 feet wide at its tip. Sitting in the boardroom as the OCC director reeled off a 'bill of particulars' would prove strikingly similar to sitting in the boardroom of the Federal Reserve Bank of Richmond just after I became chairman of Bank of America, with Jeff Lacker reciting his concerns about the bank in no uncertain terms and issuing a mandatory plan of action, except that in Chicago, we were meeting as the full board and I was not the chairman. I was just one participant on the board.

May 1st, 2009, was a warm, clear day in Richmond. Inside the Fed tower, which was imposing with its aluminum façade and breathtaking view of the James River, however, the fine weather was no balm for Frank Bramble, Charles Rossotti, Tom May, and me. We talked about our next moves in tones punctuated with the very anxiety that creased our faces. I was as anxious as my colleagues, perhaps a bit more so since, because, as Jeff Lacker had said, I would be the one everyone would be looking at.

I felt ready to do what needed to be done. I was very anxious and nervous, but I told myself I simply had to push through. I had done it before, and I could do it again. That, perhaps, was the cardinal lesson of my crisis experiences: you keep moving ahead. You keep taking the next steps, confident that you will learn as you progress. Much like in physics, where you work through a complex problem in steps, not always seeing the end immediately but having the confidence to accept that if each step, if each move is correct, you will arrive at the right solution.

Chapter Fifteen

A SERENDIPITOUS INTRODUCTION

Jeff Lacker's admonition, "the eyes of the financial community are going to be on you," continued to weigh heavily on my shoulders. In a matter of days, I would face the public as chairman of the Bank of America for the first time. In reality, at that moment, I would be facing the banking industry worldwide. The impact of my words would be far-reaching.

Committed as I was to soldiering on, I found myself reflecting on the journey with the Bank that brought me to this point.

My association with Bank of America began with an introduction that occurred sixteen years before I became its chairman. I saw nothing out of the ordinary about the introduction at the time. Only much later did I realize how serendipitous it was.

Perhaps as a physicist, I may seem an unlikely person to place much stock in the notion of serendipity. But I do. Fortuitous encounters have been a common occurrence in my life. And I can assure you that the history of physics is replete with serendipitous discoveries. German physicist Wilhelm Conrad Röntgen, for example, accidentally discovered X-rays in 1895 while testing whether cathode rays could pass through glass.

In 1990, I was nominated by then-President George H.W. Bush and confirmed by the Senate to be Director of the National Science Foundation. The NSF is the nation's largest and most significant funder of research in the basic sciences, and its director holds one of the most prestigious and most important positions in the world of science. As its head, I was a full-fledged government official, carrying a red passport instead of the dark-blue version reserved for private citizens.

One of my most memorable experiences as NSF director was helping to secure funding for the Laser Interferometry Gravitational Wave Observatory, or LIGO. This was the multi-million-dollar facility that was used to detect gravitational waves in 2016, exactly one hundred years after Einstein predicted their existence. The physicists who led this effort — Kip Thorne and Barry Barish of Caltech, and Ranier Weiss of MIT — won the Nobel Prize in physics in 2017. Shirley and I felt honored and utterly elated when we were invited as their guests to attend the ceremony in Stockholm.

It was our second time attending the Nobel ceremonies. The first was in 1988 when we were guests of our good friend Leon Lederman who won the Nobel Prize in physics that year.

In another of those serendipitous circumstances that have been a theme of my life, Jack Peltason, who was chancellor of the University of Illinois, Champaign Urbana, when I was a young, overly stressed faculty member, was now president of the University of California System. Jack gave me a call one night in mid-January 1995, saying he wanted to interest me in being considered for the position of provost and senior vice president for academic affairs for the UC system.

I had gotten to know Jack fairly well at Urbana when I had served as chairman of the Black Faculty and Staff Association and faculty advisor to the Black Students Association. He and I worked well together in some very sensitive and intense situations. I liked and respected him. I found him to be fair and sympathetic to issues of racial justice. I also thought he was a very skilled administrative leader. So, I listened to what he had to say.

"Walter, the provost, and senior vice president is the number-two position in the entire university system, and I know you would like it. A lot of people here know you or know about you and would really like to have you join us."

I must admit I was intrigued. After all, the University of California was universally recognized as the premier public university in the country, with outstanding campuses like Berkeley, UCLA, UC San Diego, and others. And it managed three very important Department of Energy national laboratories. But I wasn't sure I wanted to go to a number-two position anywhere at this point in my life and career. I was really more interested now in being a university president. In any event, I was not quite ready to leave the NSF.

I said all of this to Jack.

Without hesitation, as if he had prepared for my response, he said, "Well, you know the chancellorship of the Irvine campus is also open, and I would love to have you there. But Walter, I am seventy years old and I'm not going to be hanging around that much longer. If you were in the number two position, you would be in the catbird seat for a shot to be the next president."

This was alluring. "Let me give it some thought, Jack, and I'll call you back in a few days."

"OK. Let me know if you have any questions."

When I told Shirley about my conversation with Jack, I'm pretty sure her first thought was, "What! We're moving again!"

In our twenty years of marriage, we had moved from Chicago to Urbana, Urbana to Providence, then back to Chicago, and finally to Washington, via a six-month stay in Paris.

Now, when people ask her, "What do you do?" she replies, without the slightest trace of irony, "I am a professional mover." However, after thinking hard about it, talking to our sons and friends, and calling colleagues, we decided to make a new start and 'go west.'

Before we left for California, I had asked several of my friends and colleagues to introduce me to members of the corporate and cultural communities in the San Francisco area where I would be based. Shirley and I had served on several cultural and corporate boards in Chicago, and I wanted to continue that kind of involvement in California. I was sure that, as provost, I would meet individuals of the same ilk in those communities, but I wanted to be introduced to them before I arrived in San Francisco.

Although I had some science and academic colleagues there, the only person Shirley and I really knew well in California was Avon Kirkland, my best friend who had introduced me to Shirley. Avon had given up his career as a research chemist and head of an educational publishing company and lived in Berkeley as a television writer and producer.

I called to tell him we would be coming to the Bay area and why.

"Wow! Provost of UC! Does that mean Berkeley?" he asked.

I could feel his excitement. See his big wide smile.

"No," I said, smiling myself. "I'll be the provost of the entire system, not just the Berkeley campus. All nine campuses. And I'll oversee the three national laboratories. I'll be back in the national laboratory world again after Argonne."

"Wow! That is a big deal, Walt. Congratulations, man! You guys will love it here. And we can play tennis year-round. Do you get a residence? I think there is a provost's house in Berkeley."

"Funny you should ask. There was supposed to be a house included, but that has been removed from the deal because of budget cuts in the system."

"There are some very nice places around here. Evelyn and I will be happy to help you and Shirley look around," Avon said.

Evelyn was a prominent lawyer Avon met when he moved to California from Chicago around the same time I went to Urbana. They were now married. Reconnecting with Avon was one of the great benefits of moving to the area.

Richard 'Dick' Thomas, then CEO of The First National Bank of Chicago, was key in facilitating our introduction to California. Dick had been a senior officer of the bank when I was a board member, and he was also chairman of the board of the Chicago Symphony Orchestra (CSO). I had been a member of the CSO board before we went to Washington. Shirley and I liked being involved in the symphony and wanted to be similarly involved in San Francisco.

Before we left for California, I gave Dick a call.

He answered promptly. "Well, hello, Walter. How are things in Washington? Do you and Shirley like it there? We certainly miss both of you here in Chicago."

"Dick," I said, "That's the reason I called. We're going to be leaving in a couple of months."

"Really? I hope you are coming back to Chicago. We would love to have you back on the bank board."

"Well, unfortunately, we are not. We're going to the San Francisco area. I'm going to be provost of the University of California System."

"That's great, Walter! Congratulations! But I still wish you guys were coming back here," he said.

As much as Dick would have liked to see Shirley and me back in Chicago, I know he was genuinely happy for me. Being provost of the entire University of California system was no insignificant matter.

"Dick, one reason I am calling is to see if you could introduce me to someone at the San Francisco Symphony. I would really like to get involved with it."

"Of course," he said. "Nancy Bechtle, the president of the San Francisco Symphony, is a good friend and colleague. I'll write to her about you. I am sure she would like to have you be involved. And you should also meet Dick Rosenberg, the CEO of BankAmerica. I am going to write him and suggest that he consider you as a potential board member — if you would be interested."

"That would be fantastic, Dick! Thank you so much." I was thrilled.

Shirley and I arrived in San Francisco in April 1993. I now had one of the most influential jobs in higher education as provost of the University of California system, including oversight of the three national labs — Lawrence Berkeley and the two weapons labs, Lawrence Livermore and Los Alamos. We bought a beautiful home in the Piedmont/Montclair district in Oakland Hills, with a 'Three Bridge' view encompassing the Golden Gate, Bay, and Richmond-San Rafael bridges — a highly sought-after amenity in San Francisco's Bay area. Avon introduced me to a tennis club where I could play two or three times a week outdoors.

As was the practice in those days, Dick Thomas wrote formal letters of introduction to Nancy Bechtle and Dick Rosenberg and sent carbon copies to me. I contacted both of them when I arrived in San Francisco, and both invited me to lunch. Nancy took me to a very chic French restaurant. She was a delightful, elegant woman and was genuinely glad to meet me. Dick must have said some remarkable things about me because almost immediately, she began to talk about my joining the SFO board. And indeed, very soon after our lunch, I was formally invited to join the board. One of the most memorable experiences of being on the SFO board was meeting Michael Tilson Thomas, who was a very young conductor then, but who has turned out to be one of the most admired symphony directors in the world.

Dick Rosenberg and I met for the first time, also over lunch, but in the private dining room of BankAmerica's world headquarters, a fifty-two-story skyscraper that boasted panoramic views of downtown San Francisco and the Golden Gate Bridge. Dick did not come across as the chairman and CEO of the largest and most prestigious bank in California. A former naval commander who served in Korea and Vietnam, he was a down-to-earth, affable man. He was Jewish, born and raised in Fall River, Massachusetts, about fifteen miles from Brown University. At first, we talked a lot about that area of New England. I learned what Fall River was like for him in the days when it was one of the capitals of the fabric industry. He still had family there. Soon, he broached the real reason for our lunch date.

IN THE EYE OF THE STORM

"I spoke to Dick Thomas, and he was very complimentary of you," he said. "Would you consider joining the board of BankAmerica?"

"Of course," I replied enthusiastically.

I confess the question took me by surprise. Certainly, I had hoped to be asked to join the board. But I did not expect that to happen so quickly. In my mind, my lunch with Dick Rosenberg would be the first of several conversations. There would be a few more lunches and meetings with several people after I had been in San Francisco longer, I thought. I later learned Dick's seemingly spur-of-the-moment invitation was common in those days when the chairman of an organization was the key person in selecting board members. I recalled that it was the chairman of Amoco Oil, who had invited me to join that company's board. Still, I'm sure Dick had already spoken to the BankAmerica board about me by the time he asked me to consider becoming a director.

In looking back on moments like these, I am thankful that I have no ability to see into the future. Had I foreseen what would be thrust upon me, would I have jumped at the chance to join the BankAmerica board? I'm sure I still would have, but that's because even if I were the one doing the foreseeing, I would have regarded a prediction of my becoming chairman of the board of the country's largest bank with the hilarity it deserved. I'd have chalked it up to a momentary, mad flirtation with hubris. A joke on the mind of the physicist I was.

Shortly after my lunch with Dick Rosenberg, I received a phone call and a letter welcoming me to the board. Nowadays, selecting board members is a much more formal process, with governance committees, nominating committees, and the entire board much more involved.

The invitation to join the board of BankAmerica was a real privilege and a great honor for me. BankAmerica was a legendary institution within the banking community — nationally and internationally. It had a storied history. Founded as the Bank of Italy in 1904 by Amadeo Giannini, an immigrant financier, it was often called the "people's bank." It underwrote several major enterprises, from the movies to the wine business, that made California a great state for its citizens and for bankers. It was a bank that we at First Chicago emulated. Along with J.P. Morgan, it was probably one of the most admired banks in the country.

Joining the BankAmerica board was momentous for the University of California as well as myself. Shortly after I joined, I received a call from one of the university's regents.

"This is great, Walter. Stanford may have someone on the Wells Fargo board, but we now have someone at BankAmerica," he said gleefully.

This was not a frivolous statement. Rather, it reflected the fierce rivalry between the University of California, Berkeley, and Stanford University, both academically and athletically. Wells Fargo and BankAmerica were the biggest banks in the state, and both universities vied for their philanthropic attention. The rivalry exists to this day, even among alumni.

CHAPTER SIXTEEN

FROM BANKAMERICA
TO BANK OF AMERICA

I attended my first BankAmerica board meeting the very next month after my lunch with Dick Rosenberg. The other BankAmerica board members were very welcoming. I immediately observed that it was a much more relaxed atmosphere than what I had grown accustomed to on other boards. Here, the tone and tenor were decidedly 'Californian' — casual, despite the formalities of conducting a meeting and the very consequential issue we tackled: a potential merger for the bank.

Unlike when I joined the board of First Chicago, I now had some experience and could get up to speed faster on the issues the bank faced. I was fortunate in this regard because the banking industry was moving into a new era, with new rules and institutional behaviors. As large as BankAmerica was, it was facing a rapidly consolidating financial sector. Deregulation was a thing of the present, freeing commercial banks to operate across state boundaries, grow larger, and deal with increasingly mobile customers. Bank mergers were the order of the day.

One of the most acquisitive players was NationsBank based in Charlotte, North Carolina. NationsBank traced its roots to Commercial National Bank, established in 1874, and American Trust Company, founded in 1909. Both were headquartered in Charlotte. The two merged in 1957 to form American Commercial Bank, which, in turn, merged with Security National Bank of Greensboro, North Carolina, to form North Carolina National Bank (NCNB). From its beginnings as a small local bank, NCNB had grown through bold acquisitions, slightly larger than BankAmerica in market value. It adopted the name NationsBank. By 1995 it was the third-largest commercial banking organization in the United States, a gargantuan leap from its 29th ranking twelve years earlier. It passed BankAmerica in fifth place.

Hugh L. McColl, Jr., who became president of NCNB at thirty-eight-years-old and its CEO ten years later, led NationsBank. This is the man who would create the bank that brought Frank Bramble, Charles Rossetti, Tom May, Chad Gifford and me, before federal regulators in Virginia. His imprint on Bank of America would be indelible.

A master poker player, McColl was a legend in the industry for his drive, tenacity, ambition, and no-nonsense demeanor. He was a former officer in the United States Marine Corps and carried himself with a military bearing that belied his relatively small stature of five feet, seven inches tall. It was said that he kept a hand grenade in his office and would toy with it during meetings with subordinates. I must admit I never saw this prop. I also heard that he had hand grenades made in crystal and gave them out to employees whose performance he deemed worthy of reward.

McColl took NCNB on an aggressive expansion in the Southeast, swallowing forty-nine banks in his wake. The culture of NCNB was expansionist from its very beginning. Its strategy for growth was always by acquisition. But McColl's acquisition offensive was peerless. Some analysts said it started out as a defensive move in response to a prevailing fear at the time that New York City money center banks were aiming to 'devour' Southern banks. That may have been true, but Hugh McColl had dreams as big as the sky. The press labeled him "predatory," "voracious," "wily," "pugnacious," "brash," "the emperor of banking," and even "scorched-earth operator."

BankAmerica could not afford to ignore the consolidation wave sweeping the industry. As our own board discussed possible mergers, NationsBank seemed an obvious candidate because it complemented BankAmerica in several ways. NationsBank operated mainly in the Southeast and Texas, while BankAmerica was strong in the West and had recently acquired Continental Bank in Chicago.

NationsBank was almost entirely domestic; BankAmerica had businesses in thirty-eight foreign countries, spanning Europe, Asia, and South America. A merger of the two would create the largest commercial banking organization in the United States and the third-largest commercial banking organization in the world after Citigroup and Union Bank of Switzerland.

The business case for a merger clearly made a lot of sense. For McColl, a merger with BankAmerica would mean bragging rights for engineering what he long craved: the first ocean-to-ocean bank in the nation's history, a truly national bank.

Yet, merger negotiations often fall apart over issues that can seem unrelated to the overall corporate advantages. This is precisely what happened when NationsBank and BankAmerica tried to merge in 1995. Who will be the CEO? Where will the new headquarters be? Who will get to sit on the board? I've been through several mergers and acquisitions, and these three issues invariably arise. In this case, a fourth, equally nettlesome issue surfaced: Because the two banks were about the same size, would our union be a 'merger of equals' rather than a straight acquisition?

All of these issues had to be negotiated. Although there had been ongoing discussions between Dick Rosenberg and Hugh McColl about the benefits of combining the banks, these issues could not be resolved. The headquarters of the proposed combined bank proved especially thorny.

Two accounts of what transpired when Dick and McColl discussed merging over lunch in 1995 illustrate just how vexing this particular aspect of their negotiations was. One account is found in McColl's authorized biography, *McColl: The Man with America's Money*, written by Ross Yockey and published in 1999. In the book, Dick says to McColl, "You're crazy for wanting to stay in Charlotte. It's nowhere. It's small time ... You're pissing away an overwhelming opportunity here. There is simply no way you can achieve your personal ambitions with a company headquartered in Charlotte, North Carolina." To which, McColl responds, "Interesting offer, Dick ... A lot to think about." The men are said to have parted without "any hope in the weak handshake."

A second account is described in an interview the *San Francisco Business Times* had with Dick in 2014. Dick recounts in the interview that he and McColl shook hands over lunch on a deal to merge and establish headquarters in Chicago. But McColl did not keep up his end of the bargain on Chicago because his board would not give up Charlotte's status as headquarters, Dick states in the interview. "We had a deal. We had a handshake. The only issue was where the headquarters would be located. I spent too many years in the Navy not to respect the handshake of a Marine," the *San Francisco Business Times* quotes him as saying.

I cannot vouch for either of these exchanges, and I was not on the negotiating team for the merger. Dick did keep us informed, but I was not privy to the tone or spirit of their talks. What Dick brought back to us from his conversations with McColl, was that all of the quantitative measures for a merger seemed to exist in terms of nationwide coverage and the complementarity of the various strengths of each entity and that it seemed to be an excellent fit.

"Why, then, hadn't the deal proceeded to the finish line?"

That question hung stubbornly in the air until we came up with answers. First, a BankAmerica-NationsBank merger would break new ground. There had never been a financial merger of this size in the history of the country. But the idea of a leviathan created with the speed of a merger agreement did not sit well with everyone in BankAmerica's executive suite. David Coulter, the bank's president at the time, let it be known that he would rather concentrate on growing BankAmerica on its own. He preferred a go-slow approach to expansion.

Second, a huge part of the merger conversation revolved around two points: Who would be the CEO, and where the headquarters would be. Those were the issues the board talked about. This was both fascinating and puzzling to me.

"Why would two things like that be so important?" I kept asking myself.

Over the years, I learned that where CEOs want to live can be an important issue in where the headquarters of the corporations wind up. None of us on the board thought it made sense to go to Charlotte, North Carolina. The places we talked about were Chicago and Atlanta. And given BankAmerica's historic association with San Francisco, it was difficult to agree to move elsewhere, especially to a smaller city like Charlotte.

Very few of the BankAmerica directors, including me, had ever even been to Charlotte. We considered Chicago because we owned Continental Bank there, and it was a financial center in the middle of the country. Atlanta was considered because it was a metropolitan area, BankAmerica had corporate clients there, and NationsBank had a major presence there. Dick did not seem wedded to either of these cities. He was more concerned about placing the headquarters where it would be good for business.

I did not know then that moving the headquarters to Charlotte would be good for me.

Shirley and I were loving California. I really enjoyed the UC system and my new colleagues. But I learned very quickly that not all was wine and roses in the Golden State. In 1994, the issue of affirmative action began to be debated in a heightened manner throughout the state and throughout the university system. It ultimately became a defining issue for the university. Were it not for a string of circumstances that coalesced during that time, Shirley and I might have spent the rest of our lives enjoying the California sunshine, and it's beautiful views.

So, what happened? Why did we stay for just a little over two years?

The concatenation of circumstances included my changing feelings about the job of provost and even the possible presidency. Attitudes toward affirmative action were also changing in the state and in the university, with ongoing debates as to whether or not all such programs in the university system should be abolished. And, most unexpectedly, Morehouse College reappeared on the scene.

CHAPTER SEVENTEEN

THE SEDUCTION OF A MOREHOUSE PRESIDENCY

I came home from work one day in early January of 1995, and before I could say hello to Shirley, I heard her speaking loudly on the phone.

"No! That is not going to happen! We just got here. I know they would like Walter to co…" She broke off momentarily when she saw me and then continued in a rush, dropping her voice to its normal pitch. "Oh, here is Walter. I've got to go now. Yes, yes! I'll say hello to him from you."

She hung up — a little too hurriedly, I thought — and turned to me with a smile. "Oh, hi. How are you? How was your day?

"Good, good," I said quickly. "Who was that? And what was that all about?"

"Haven't you heard? Roy Keith has been asked to resign from the presidency at Morehouse."

"Yes, yes. I heard that somewhere. So?"

"Well, that was Lynne Edmonds, saying everyone is talking about getting you to go to Morehouse as president."

"What! Are they crazy? We have only been here a little over a year. Besides, I am not that big on going back south. It took me long enough to get away from there. Forget it!"

"That's what I told her."

She said that with finality, indicating the discussion was over as far as she was concerned.

It really was. Shirley's next words were, "What are we going to do for dinner? Do you want to go out?"

Lynne and David Edmonds were one of our oldest 'couple friends.' They had four sons, two of whom had gone to Morehouse. Lynne stayed plugged into the Morehouse network. We met them when we were all young faculty members and administrators at Brown University.

Shirley and I did go out to dinner that night, to Crogan's, a little seafood restaurant a few blocks from our house that was a favorite of ours. There wasn't anything particularly fancy about Crogan's. No white tablecloths or über-chef presentations for this Irish-American neighborhood spot, with its pub-like, home-style fare, including my favorite, Linguine con Vongole (Linguine with Clams). We just liked the food, the service, the atmosphere, and the prices were right.

"Boy, that's weird," I said during dinner. "They really think we would move to Atlanta, and you have never even lived in the south. Lynne knows that."

"True. And I'm not sure I would like living there," Shirley said. She had accompanied me to my 20th Morehouse College reunion in 1978 and had said at the time that she had 'mixed feelings' about Atlanta.

"Well, I can't believe they really expect you to come back," Shirley said.

"Yeah. This will blow over; I'm pretty sure. And they will find someone pretty quickly," I said.

It didn't blow over. Calls kept coming to us from alumni, old friends, faculty members, trustees, and the professional headhunter that the school had hired. I meanwhile, felt satisfied and was enjoying my life and job.

Yet, something was missing. Being in the system-wide office was not like being on a campus. The offices were in a high-rise building in downtown Oakland, along with commercial businesses, including insurance companies and law offices.

I did visit all the campuses on a regular basis, and they are all beautiful, albeit in different ways. Berkeley is like an old New England campus; UCLA is in a bucolic, lush, green, and flowery upscale neighborhood; and Santa Cruz is nestled in a redwood forest with spectacular ocean views. But I spent much of my time in Sacramento, the state capital, dealing with the legislature and the governor's office on budgetary and governance issues. Whenever I visited a campus, I would think, "the Chancellors on the campuses are the ones having all the fun. They have students, football and basketball teams, and tennis teams, as well as alumni, and they live in nice houses right on the campus."

Maybe I should have taken the Irvine position, I sometimes mused.

Meanwhile, calls about Morehouse kept coming in. One, in particular, made all the difference. It came one evening in late January.

"Hey, Walt! It's John here. How are you doing, man?" It was my close friend, John Hopps. John and I were freshman roommates in Graves Hall at Morehouse, and we both went on to get our Ph.D. in physics. John had been very successful in his career and was now deputy director of the Draper Laboratory at MIT. We had stayed in close touch but hadn't spoken for quite a while.

"John! Wow! So glad to hear from you! How's June? And the kids?" I was genuinely delighted to hear from him.

"They're great. I just spoke to Junie, and she knows I'm calling you," he said.

I said, "Oh, OK. Is this about Morehouse?" I was almost certain this was the reason for his call, given its timing, and just wanted him to confirm it.

"Yeah, it is. And I am going to fly out and talk with you about it. OK?"

"What! You are coming all the way from Boston to talk with me about Morehouse!" I didn't expect this at all.

"Yep! Yep! I think I need to do that, OK?" He wasn't really asking.

"Well, sure. If you think so," I replied.

"OK. What about the day after tomorrow? Can we have dinner?"

"Yeah, OK. Here's our address."

Two days later, John Hopps and I were having dinner at Crogan's. He gave me a detailed account of what he thought was happening at the college. The situation clearly was precarious, and John explained how I could really make a difference. I was moved as we both reminisced about our time at Morehouse and how much that experience had meant to us, how it changed our lives. John was also a Ford Foundation Scholar like me. And then John said something that almost brought me to tears.

"Walt, they really need you, and the alumni are ready to pitch in and help in any way they can. And if you go, I will quit my job at MIT and go with you and serve in any capacity you need me to."

I sat motionless, staring at him and thinking, "Wow! Now I have to take this very seriously."

"Does June know what you are saying?" I said after what seemed like a full minute.

"Oh yeah. We talked about it, and she is one-hundred-percent on board," he said.

John and June had met when she was at Spelman College, and we were at Morehouse. Spelman and Morehouse are 'brother/sister,' all-male, all-female colleges, respectively, located across the street from each other. John and June were one of the hundreds of Spelman-Morehouse marriages. June loved Morehouse as much as John and I did. June was now a very distinguished scholar and Dean of the School of Social Work at Boston College.

I told Shirley about John's offer later that evening. "I think we need to think again about all this," I said.

To my surprise, she said, "Yes. I have already been doing that. When you get back from Chicago, let's go over things."

I had to go to Chicago the next day for an Amoco board meeting. I returned home two days later, only to find our two sons, Keith and Eric, in the living room.

"What on earth are you guys doing here?"

I was surprised but certainly happy to see them. Keith lived in Boulder, Colorado, and Eric lived in Chicago. I found them sitting in front of our big fireplace. They smiled broadly, enjoying my surprise.

"What are you guys doing here?' I said again.

At first, I thought that something was wrong, but I quickly dismissed that thought. They wouldn't be smiling like that if there was bad news. For some reason, I did not connect them being there to Morehouse.

Keith spoke up. "Mom said we needed to come because you and she wanted to talk about whether you guys should go to Morehouse."

I was very touched by this gesture on Shirley's part and thankful that our sons were willing to take part in our decision. It was a very big decision. I would be abandoning the possibility of being president of a major research University, and it would probably mean moving out of the world of big science and national science policy forums. I would be going to a small liberal arts college with no serious research capacity, located in the very region from which I had struggled to escape. This could be the biggest decision I — we — would ever make in my entire professional career.

I recalled the warning of a very close friend, Marty Granoff when I spoke to him about Morehouse. Marty had been a big supporter of mine when I was a finalist for the presidency of Brown University in 1988, along with Vartan Gregorian (who got the job). He said, "Walter, I still have hopes that we can get you back to Brown, and I'll support you wherever you go. But you realize this probably means the end of any possibilities at Brown or similar institutions."

Marty was a trustee of Brown then.

Our sons had differing opinions. Keith was somewhat neutral, but on the whole, he felt that the presidency of the University of California was just too important a position not to pursue. Eric, our younger son, agreed that the presidency of UC was indeed very important, and pointed out that it would be historic to be the first Black person in such a position. But he argued that I could make a bigger difference in the lives of young African-Americans and in the African-American community by going back to Morehouse.

We had a spirited discussion, much of it over dinner at Crogan's, where I had a very cold Martini.

What tipped the scale in favor of Morehouse may be a conversation I had later that week with my very good friend, Vernon Jordan, who had been a mentor and advisor to me for years. Vernon was an attorney, a highly influential civil rights activist, and a close adviser to President Bill Clinton. I called him from my office at UC. Just as I was beginning to explain why I called, he interjected in that resonant, Baptist-preacher voice. "Dr. Massey," which is how he addressed me when he was half-joking, "Yes, I've heard all about it. I know they want you back at 'The House.'"

'The House,' of course, was Morehouse. Vernon always knew what was going on in the black community and especially in Atlanta, where he was from. Before we got to the meat of our conversation, we spoke briefly about family and friends. Then Vernon switched to the sonorous tone he reserved for serious matters.

"Walter, you have to go to Morehouse," he said emphatically. "They need you. And it is where you need to be."

He told me to go and read the biblical passage, Isaiah, chapter six, verse eight. I didn't have a bible in the office, but as soon as I got home that night, I rushed to read the verse. It says,

"Also, I heard the voice of the Lord saying, Whom shall I send, and who will go for us?" Then said I, 'Here am I. Send me.'"

A few days later, I learned the search committee for the UC presidency would be holding its first meeting that morning,

February 21st. Early in January, Jack Peltason had officially announced that he would be retiring at the end of the academic year. I knew my name would be in the hopper, but I had already decided to go to Morehouse. So, on the morning of February 21, I telephoned the room where the search committee was just about to meet and asked to speak to the board secretary, Leigh Trivette, who had become a colleague and good friend. When she came on the phone, I asked her to tell the committee chairman, Regent Roy Brophy, that I did not wish to be a candidate for the UC presidency. I knew that Roy had expected me to be a strong candidate. He had told me as much. And I knew I startled Leigh with my request.

"Walter, are you sure you want to do this? Why don't you just wait a while and see what happens." She sounded quite distressed.

I said, "Yes, I am sure, and I will tell you, when I see you, why I am doing this."

So, by the time the Regents of the University of California held their fateful meeting on July 20th, where they voted to abolish all affirmative action programs in hiring and admissions, it was well known that I would be leaving in August to go to Morehouse as the ninth president of the college.

Even now, my decision to go to Morehouse is the best I have ever made in my professional life, and Shirley agrees. We fell happily into a busy life, reconnecting with black society, black workplaces, and other black institutions in ways we had not done in years, having spent all of our married life in predominantly white institutions.

Going to Morehouse also put Shirley and me on campus, in a new home built for the president and first lady (the formal title of the president's wife), which meant we interacted with the students, the community, and faculty on a daily basis. We also made many new friends who included some very famous people, like film director-producer-actor, Spike Lee, and actor Samuel L. Jackson, both Morehouse alums; actor Denzel Washington, whose son was attending Morehouse; record producer Quincy

Jones; and media icon-philanthropist Oprah Winfrey, who became Morehouse's largest donor. The most important thing we did was preside over the education and graduation of more than five thousand young African American men, Morehouse Men, who have gone on to make a tremendous difference in all walks of society.

We loved the entire experience. There were challenges, to be sure, but there were joys also. Grim, even maddening moments and moments of sheer elation — these are worthy of description in a tome of their own.

CHAPTER EIGHTEEN
MEETING THE BOFA CEO

It wasn't until 1998 that NationsBank and BankAmerica reached an agreement to merge. We announced our $62.5 billion merger on April 14th that year. But just a few days before we made the announcement, the Travelers Group Inc. and Citicorp announced their own merger in a $74 billion deal that created Citigroup Inc. That made our NationsBank-BankAmerica merger the second largest at the time, which was disappointing from a superlative ego perspective, but validated our view about the need for consolidation in the industry and made our decision to merge with NationsBank seem even more appropriate.

Charlotte would be the new corporate home of our combined bank. McColl had won. This was his crowning achievement. We knew, and so did the entire industry, that it no longer was a merger of equals. Rather, it was a takeover of BankAmerica by NationsBank. This was NationsBank's M.O. under McColl.

"We never think about giving up control of anything," he told reporters.

Dick stated to the board and publicly that the merger was a far cry from the deal he and Hugh had discussed in 1995.

"It was a very different deal. The deal in 1998 may have been billed as a merger, but it was really an acquisition of Bank of America by NationsBank," he said at a press conference years later.

Yet, the new entity took the name with better clout, better cachet — Bank of America. Interestingly, this had been the historic name of BankAmerica until it was changed around 1956 with the establishment of BankAmerica Corporation as the holding company of Bank of America and its subsidiaries at the time.

In late 2019, I had lunch with a colleague from Bank of America who had started out as a young analyst at the old North Carolina National Bank (NCNB) in the 1980s, working directly with Hugh McColl. He told me the following story, which he swore to be true. Just after NCNB acquired First Republic Bank in Texas in 1988, several people at an NCNB management meeting suggested to Hugh that the bank needed a less parochial name — a name that indicated it was no longer just a regional North Carolina institution, but a truly national bank. Hugh agreed but said he wasn't quite ready to make a change.

"Well, if we *did* make a change, do you have any idea what you would like it to be called?" someone asked Hugh, according to the story.

Hugh paused for a moment, and then said, "Bank of America."

It took ten years, but Hugh finally got the name he wanted.

The Bank of America of 1998 held $572 billion in assets and would operate approximately 4,800 full-service branches in 27 states and 38 countries, and more than 14,000 ATMs nationwide. By the time the deal won regulatory approval in October, its value had fallen to $37 billion from $62.5 billion announced in April because of a drop in the price of NationsBank shares. U.S. bank stocks were being battered by problems in Asian and European markets at the time.

Besides agreeing to locate the headquarters in Charlotte, the new board also elected Hugh McColl chairman and CEO of the new Bank of America. NationsBank's directors held a majority of thirteen seats — twelve directors, plus the chairman's seat — of the twenty-four on the board. The chairman-CEO's seat was viewed as distinct from the others. It was awarded to NationsBank because Hugh McColl was chosen chairman and CEO of the combined bank. On our side, there were eleven directors. The 12-11 split in NationsBank's favor was consistent with the relative value of the banks' stocks at the time.

Despite accounts suggesting acrimony between Dick and Hugh in their initial merger talks, Dick remained on the board. He and Hugh were very professional in their interactions and appeared to get along with each other.

I certainly hoped to serve on the new board, but I was not sure I would be among the directors chosen from the old BankAmerica. The decision, I assumed, rested with Hugh McColl.

In June, Hugh visited Atlanta to give a luncheon talk, and I attended. After the talk, he pulled me aside.

"I'd like to set up a time to talk with you, Walter," he said.

"Of course," I replied.

I got a call from his office a few days later. He wanted to come to Morehouse to see me. When I told this to Shirley, she declared that she, too, would be there when he arrived.

"I want to meet the man I've heard so much about," she said flatly.

Hugh came into my outer office on the appointed day, accompanied by a very large African-American gentleman. To my surprise, Shirley blurted out, "Oh! You are short, like my husband." She hadn't even said hello.

Hugh stared at her, bemused. Thankfully, the ensuing silence was brief. Shirley broke it, of course.

"Hi. I am Shirley Massey, Walter's wife," Shirley said, extending her hand to Hugh.

Hugh smiled, shook her hand warmly, chatted a bit, and then he and I went into my private office.

After chatting for a few minutes, Hugh said, "I came here to ask if you would be willing to continue as a director on the board of the merged bank."

"Of course. I would like to," I said. I know I sounded calm, but inwardly I was very excited.

In fact, I was thrilled. We had a fairly long talk after that. Hugh shared his thoughts on how he saw the merger coming along and what he expected to happen. It was all quite positive. I really appreciated his coming to see me in person. I don't know if he did that with all of the directors.

The large African-American gentleman turned out to be Hugh's bodyguard, and the ex-husband of my receptionist, Barbara Wardlaw. I did not learn of Barbara's connection to him until she told us after he and Hugh had left.

What a small world, I thought.

Little did I know then, from the time I was introduced to Dick Rosenberg, I had embarked on a journey toward the chairmanship of the Bank of America board. Hugh's visit to Morehouse had taken me several more steps on that journey.

It seemed reasonable that the chief of the combined bank would be the more experienced Hugh McColl. At BankAmerica, David Coulter, who succeeded Dick Rosenberg as our chairman and CEO in 1996, was fairly new. He was named president of the new Bank of America with the 'understanding' that he would become CEO when McColl retired at sixty-five years old. Coulter would be fifty-two at that time.

Not a word of this 'understanding' was enshrined in a formal agreement, and it never came to pass.

At the time of the merger, Hugh had two trusted lieutenants, Ken Lewis and James Hanson. Within NationsBank, and within the industry, it was widely assumed prior to the merger that either Ken Lewis or Jim Hanson, and not Dave Coulter, would be Hugh's eventual successor.

One day, a few weeks after the merger was completed, I got a call from David Coulter's assistant, Cindy, informing me that Dave had been asked to leave the bank. I was traveling when she reached me.

"Walter, do you have a few minutes to talk? I'm calling about Dave."

"Sure."

"You're going to read about this. Dave is going to be leaving the board *and* the bank."

"Really? Why?" I was genuinely shocked. After all, we had a gentleman's agreement that David would be groomed as Hugh's successor. It was one of the reasons why we agreed to have Hugh serve as chair. David had succeeded Dick as BankAmerica's chairman and CEO, which logically positioned him for the chairman-chief executive position of the combined bank once Hugh retired. So, I was floored when Cindy said he was leaving the bank altogether.

"We've heard the executive committee of the board has asked him to step down," Cindy said.

Apparently, Hugh McColl and the board's new executive committee, chaired by William "Hootie" Johnson that made up of a majority of former NationsBank directors, had demanded David's departure. "Hootie" Johnson was a longtime confidant of McColl. A former head of Banker's Trust of South Carolina, he was, like McColl, Southern born and bred, the son of a banker, and unapologetically bank-acquisitive. But he probably was best known as the chairman of the exclusive Augusta National Golf Club (host of the Master's Tournament) who declared in 2002 that the club would not admit women "at the point of a bayonet."

At McColl's behest, Johnson flew to San Francisco from Charlotte to demand David's resignation in person. They blamed David for a $372 million write-off BankAmerica was forced to take on its exposure to D.E. Shaw & Company, a Wall Street hedge fund that managed a high-risk trading operation. The unexpected write-off slashed our third-quarter profits in half, infuriating McColl and his Charlotte team. The investment in Shaw was made under David's watch prior to the merger with NationsBank.

The head that rolled was David's.

He 'retired' on October 30th, twenty days after the merger was complete. There had been no formal meeting to discuss his case. It's quite likely that David spoke privately to some of his strongest BankAmerica supporters about what had led to his 'retirement,' including the Shaw investment and Johnson's visit, but I had no such conversation with him or with BankAmerica board members. In fact, the next time I saw all of the BankAmerica directors who remained on the new board was in Charlotte at the first meeting of that board on October 28th.

David's departure left us in shock. Some of us chatted about it quietly among ourselves — mostly one-on-one instead of in a group. Our general feeling was that Hugh and his colleagues on the board had railroaded David. It seemed obvious to all of us that the Shaw debacle was a convenient excuse to remove him as a potential successor to Hugh. David had a stellar record until then. He had overseen the acquisition of Chicago-based Continental Bank Corporation in a $2 billion deal that made BankAmerica the largest corporate lender in the United States at the time, and BankAmerica's profits rose every quarter and its stock tripled while he was CEO.

Our shock soon gave way to indignation. We voiced our feelings, albeit quietly. Typical comments were:

"This is no resignation. It's a firing! They wanted a reason to get David out of the picture, and they used Shaw."

"Did they even consider all the great things Dave did for BankAmerica?"

"David's days were numbered from the get-go! He suffered the same fate as CEOs in other banks that merged with NationsBank."

"Dave was no match for McColl."

"Shouldn't they have talked with us before they fired Dave?"

But all the mutterings, hurt feelings, and resentments came to naught. The newly merged bank was going to be run by the NationsBank team, including McColl and whoever would become his successor, and that was that!

David was more than a colleague to me, and I experienced a sense of loss after his departure. I had gotten to know him as a friend because he was the only other tennis player on the board beside me. When the board went on retreats, Dave and I would head to the tennis courts while the others played golf. I found it remarkable that he seemed to bear little anger over the circumstances of his resignation, at least in public. I never heard him disparage McColl or Johnson. He remained in good spirits until his departure. He was disappointed, I'm sure, but he moved on with his life.

I saw him several times after he left the bank, and his life truly was exciting. After leaving Bank of America, he joined Beacon Group L.P., a small investment firm that J.P. Morgan Chase, the country's second-largest bank, acquired in 2000. The acquisition landed Dave in the plum position of executive chairman of J.P. Morgan Chase's investment banking unit. I was very pleased for him.

CHAPTER NINETEEN
THE NEW BANK OF AMERICA

The cultures of BankAmerica and NationsBank were as different as night and day. From the board perspective, NationsBank's was a buttoned-down, staid, and formal world, and there was never any doubt about who was in charge: Hugh McColl. On the other hand, BankAmerica's was a put-your-feet-up, jackets-off, California-relaxed domain with lots of questioning and discussion.

At BankAmerica it was not uncommon to see cheerful spouses and partners at dinners and retreats. At occasional parties in the evenings after board meetings, several of us, board members and officers would go dancing at local clubs. At NationsBank, spouses were never invited to retreats or parties. There were no parties anyway, and certainly no dancing.

Inevitably, the differences in corporate cultures led to some friction. Some in the legacy BankAmerica camp still bristled over the ouster of Dave Coulter and the fact that we were subordinated to NationsBank in the merger. But this did not manifest itself in any untoward way on the board. There, the difference was more a matter of style — buttoned-down versus casual. Buttoned-down triumphed. Everyone's conduct at meetings was very professional. We got things done. Was it worth the while to grouse over the fact that the composition of the board and the senior leadership worked in favor of whatever the chairman desired? I didn't think so. We had agreed to it, and the business was doing well.

Personally, the newly combined bank proved beneficial to me in a very important way. I was now living in Atlanta, where I was president of Morehouse College. Before the merger, I had been traveling to San Francisco for board meetings, which consumed a lot of my time. Commuting to Charlotte for meetings was much more convenient than traveling to San Francisco.

Atlanta was more enjoyable than Shirley and I had anticipated, and being president of Morehouse College was a bigger deal than we expected. We were getting used to being (back for me) in the south. It was nothing like when I left after graduating from Morehouse. A major difference was the number of black people in prominent positions — so many more than anywhere we had lived, and many of them were Morehouse and Spelman alumni. Maynard Jackson, the first African American mayor of Atlanta, was a fellow student at Morehouse, and like me, a Ford Foundation Scholar. He was now a member of the Morehouse College Board of Trustees and a very good friend.

All of our doctors, lawyers, dentists, and accountants were Morehouse alumni —"Morehouse Men" — and so Shirley and I were well looked after in every regard. This proved a blessing at a particularly frightening time.

I call it "the time of my miracle."

We lived in the newly built president's residence on campus, named "Davidson House" after the family of alum Robert Davidson that donated much of the money for its construction. After a football game one evening, Shirley and I were entertaining a few parents and alumni on our screened-in patio when one of our guests, physician John Williams, said to me, "Doc, you have been coughing a lot today. Why don't you come by the office tomorrow for an X-ray, just to make sure everything is okay?"

"Really?" I said. "I don't think it's anything."

"Well, let's just make sure. It will only take a few minutes."
I agreed to see him first thing the next morning.

I went for the X-ray and thought no more about it until the following evening when Dr. Williams called. He had shown my X-ray to some of his colleagues.

"We think you should go to see Doctor Joe Miller over at Emory University."

"Why?" I was concerned but not alarmed.

"There are some spots we don't understand, and he is the leading lung specialist in the city."

I was beginning to be a little more than just concerned now. I told Shirley about the call, and the next day I went to see Dr. Miller, who turned out to be an affable, somewhat older white gentleman. Not a Morehouse Man as I had expected. He ordered new X-rays, and he showed me the results.

"Do you see those spots?" He pointed to the screen.

"Yes."

"Well, they have broadened from where they were on the first X-ray that Dr. Williams sent me."

"What does that mean?"

"I'm not exactly sure, but it's unusual. Have you been around barnyard animals or anywhere you might have picked up a fungus?"

"No. I haven't been anywhere like that."

"We're going to do a CAT scan just to be sure. I'll get it scheduled right away."

I was growing more worried. "Are you saying it might be cancer?"

"It could be," Dr. Miller said gently. "I can't rule that out. But let's wait for the results. And maybe you should bring your wife with you when we go over the results."

Now I was *really* worried. I didn't want to upset Shirley, so I just asked her to go with me the next day without saying Dr. Miller had suggested it.

In his office, a typically small room, Dr. Miller pointed to printouts of my X-rays and CAT scan results and said,

"We have to assume it probably is cancer, but maybe not malignant. In any case, we ought to take a biopsy and plan for treatment before it spreads."

Shirley and I took in Dr. Miller's words more calmly than I would have thought. I'm not sure what I felt, but it wasn't panic. I suppose I was more resigned than anything else. My attitude was, "Well, I guess it's my turn to have something serious happen."

Dr. Miller said, "I will schedule the biopsy to test for malignancy and to isolate the precise location for treatment."

He proceeded to expound on the very small chances of the lung being punctured by the biopsy needle, and on all the other very rare horrible things that could happen. I tuned him out.

It all began to sink in that night. I could not relax. Dire thoughts pummeled me mercilessly. *I have lung cancer and could die. What will happen to Shirley? So many things I want to do. I want to see our grandchildren as they grow up.*

Filled with gloom, which I was determined to hide from Shirley, I turned to the chairman of my Board of Trustees, the Rev. Otis Moss, Jr.

Otis and I were students together at Morehouse. He became a major figure in the Civil Rights Movement, working directly with the Rev. Dr. Martin Luther King, Jr., and was now the pastor of a prestigious Church in Cleveland. I had not been a 'church-going' person since I graduated from Morehouse, but I loved to hear Otis preach. I now thought of him as someone I could speak with, not just as my Chairman (effectively my boss), but also as a friend and counselor.

I phoned him the same evening after Shirley had gone to bed. I went straight to the point.

"Otis, it seems that I most likely have lung cancer."

I told him everything — from Dr. Williams' observation on the patio to Dr. Miller's conclusions. Otis was most comforting. He assured me that I had plenty of support and that he and the Morehouse community would help me through whatever happened.

I will never forget his words. They were so soothing that they brought me to tears. "It's going to be all right, Massey. We will work through this together." He always called me by my last name.

Two days later, I was in a hospital bed at Emory University Hospital, awaiting a CAT scan to determine precisely where the needle should be inserted before I was sedated for the biopsy. Shirley had gone for a walk. She'd said she would be back before I came out of sedation. Typical of her thoughtfulness, she had brought a ham sandwich (my favorite), so I would have something to eat when I regained consciousness. I had not been allowed to eat anything since the night before.

I was feeling pretty calm, still resigned to whatever was to be, when I was inserted into a CAT scan capsule. I could still hear the technician.

"Are you okay, Mr. Massey? We are about to start."

"Yes. Yes, I am."

I heard the exchange between the technician and someone named Steve, who I assumed was his assistant.

"Okay, Steve. What are the coordinates?"

"They should be right on the X-ray we just took."

"I don't see anything on the X-ray. Are you sure?"

"Yes, I am sure."

"Let me call Dr. Miller's office and make sure we have the right X-rays."

I heard only the technician's side of the phone call, of course. "Well, there are no spots on the X-ray...Yes, it says Walter Massey, birthday April 5th, 1938 ... Well, OK."

The technician hung up and rolled me out of the capsule. "There's nothing on your lungs that we can see," he said.

I didn't know what to think. I didn't know how to feel. I didn't know whether to be excited or relieved. I was wheeled back to my room. A nurse and doctor came in and told me whatever the first X-ray showed had disappeared, and Dr. Miller said I could go home.

I called Shirley and told her to come immediately. I was ready to leave and would explain later, I said.

"Have they finished already? That was fast. Is everything OK?"

"Yes! Yes! You won't believe it!" I practically screamed into the phone.

She arrived in no time, and I ate the best ham sandwich I ever remembered having.

I don't believe in miracles. But Otis Moss, Jr., does, and maybe that's all that mattered.

Naturally, I resumed all my duties with the vigor of someone who had been given a new lease on life. Bank of America was one of the most enjoyable.

Being on the new Bank of America board gave me a seat at the very pinnacle of high finance. I was excited to be a witness to, and as far as my directorship allowed, a participant in the maneuverings at the top of the country's banking industry. It was a high-voltage period, and I was learning a lot. Expectations diverged, personalities clashed, cultures collided as Hugh McColl sought to make the marriage between NationsBank and BankAmerica work.

Shirley was quick to pick up on my high energy level when I returned home from board meetings in Charlotte. She would choose just the right moment after I had settled in from the trip to ply me with questions.

"When am I going to meet the new board members? What are they like? Why don't I ever go to Charlotte with you? I used to go to San Francisco."

She was used to the old BankAmerica board's easy socializing, with spouses invited to retreats and post-meeting parties and dinners. Moreover, she had met Hugh McColl when he visited Atlanta and liked him. His outgoing, hearty manner certainly suggested great synergy with the social footprint of BankAmerica's board. This couldn't be further from the truth.

"Well, it's not like San Francisco. There is no dancing after the meetings. And when I am in meetings, there is nothing for you to do in Charlotte," I told Shirley.

130

And there wasn't. This was a new order. Typically, Shirley took it in stride.

Nevertheless, I felt that I fit in very well with my new bank colleagues. Better, in some ways, than my fellow directors from California because I was a southerner and understood the culture. I was one of only two African-Americans on the board. The other was Ron Townsend, a former president of the Gannett Television Group, who was on the old NationsBank board. Ron was a southerner himself and was the first Black member of the Augusta National Golf Club, so he knew Hootie and Hugh very well.

Race is very important and divisive in the South, and the culture of NationsBank, and Charlotte was definitely Southern. The fact that there were only two African-Americans on the board, however, was not unique to the South. I was the only African-American on the BankAmerica board. The rarity of African-Americans in boardrooms nationwide was — and remains — a national, not a Southern issue.

Like Hugh, who was born in Bennettsville, South Carolina, and schooled in the South — he graduated from the University of North Carolina at Chapel Hill with a degree in business administration. I was a Southerner by birth and culture and shared some of the cultural norms and references that often transcend race: speech patterns, food preferences, hunting, fishing, and religion. Southerners didn't drink spirits during the day. We drank sweet tea. But in California, everyone had wine at lunch. Activities like hunting, fishing, and quail shooting weren't part of the lifestyle of many of our California colleagues. Because we mingled socially very little at the new Bank of America, it wasn't easy to get to know senior management on a personal level. We had one early outing in Arizona shortly after the merger, but that was it.

Contrary to his tough image, I found Hugh McColl very likable, with a quick wit and a wonderful sense of humor. Later, when I invited him to Morehouse to speak to students and faculty, he mingled easily and spoke well about leadership and team building. Students and faculty all seemed to enjoy his company. I learned that he had a reputation for judging people by their performance and less by their class or race.

I never consciously delved into his life outside banking. But I learned of his role in driving affirmative action at NCNB. And that was in the early 1970s when the ink on the Equal Employment Opportunity Act was barely dry. He was also very engaged in supporting Historically Black Colleges in North Carolina.

Before long, the shine on the merger began to lose some of its brilliance. We found ourselves grappling with problem loans, a drop in its stock price, tumbling profits — all as the economy shifted into sloth drive. The board knew that Hugh planned to retire in 1999, just one year after the merger was completed. But with the industry's tongue still wagging — and with the media in lockstep — over David Coulter's surprise resignation and the bank's troubling earnings reports, the board asked him to stick around until the end of June 2002. He was game, but he stayed only until April 25, 2001, the last day he chaired the bank's annual meeting. Hundreds of shareholders showed up on that day to bid him farewell.

"When I walk off this stage today, I will do so with the knowledge that we have in place the best franchise and the best team, and I leave confident that they will produce the results which will reward our shareholders and themselves," he told the gathering as he handed the reins to Ken Lewis.

I learned a lot about Hugh, Ken, and other 'NationsBank' board members from conversations with Jackie Ward, who was a continuing member from NationsBank. Jackie, as co-founder, president, and chief executive of an information technology company, was a self-made billionaire. She was one of the most colorful people I had ever met. We traveled together from Atlanta to Charlotte on a bank plane for board meetings. She was a born and bred Southerner, with a real deep Southern accent. We became close. She would turn out to be an invaluable asset to me during the early days of my chairmanship.

As my colleagues and I prepared to leave the Virginia Fed, I began to brace myself for my all-important date with the public and the financial community. It was a mere six days away. I thought of the confidence and optimism that Hugh McColl exuded even on his last day as Bank of America's chairman and CEO and wondered if his era at the bank would inform the imprint of my chairmanship.

Chapter Twenty

PREPPING FOR MY FIRST HURDLE AS CHAIRMAN

On Friday, May 1st, 2009, the country was abuzz with the news that U.S. Supreme Court Justice David Souter would retire at the end of the Court's term in June. Souter was appointed by President George H. W. Bush, and his departure would give then-President Barack Obama an opportunity to put his own person on the bench. In a political climate fraught with partisan enmity, this was a really big deal.

But in Richmond, Virginia, on that day, our Bank of America group had paid no mind to the political bombshell of Justice Souter's retirement. After our meeting with the regulators, our group had stayed around to get our bearings and strategize. In situations like this, I've found that one usually acts on instinct based on experience. I believe the five of us did just that, as the initial shock of the revelations by Jeff Lacker and his team subsided.

My own first impulse had been to organize us. We absolutely needed to create a group or committee to oversee the implementation of the action items required by the feds. It seemed clear to us that this 'special committee' should include our small group. But there was no time to go through the process of adding others to our group. Later on, we were authorized by the board to be the Special Committee, but at that time, we were a nameless group.

Our most immediate tasks were to call Ken Lewis to give him the highlights of what had transpired and arrange to meet with him in person in Charlotte, meet with Ed Herlihy as soon as possible to engage him as an adviser to our group, brief the board by phone, and prepare a press release in response to the findings of the 'Stress Test' that federal regulators had conducted on the bank. The press release would be my first public statement as chairman of Bank of America. Understandably, of all the immediate tasks we identified, I was most anxious about this one, given Jeff Lacker's strong admonition that all eyes would be on me when it was released.

It was well after five at the height of the local rush hour, when one-by-one, depending on our travel schedules, we left the Fed building for our respective destinations.

I called Ken Lewis before I left for the airport to head back to Chicago. It was difficult to adequately convey the gravity and shock of the meeting in a fairly brief phone call, but I felt Ken understood the point I was trying to make: this was very serious and somewhat scary. I did muster a little humor, just to relieve my tension.

I said, "So Ken, I thought you said this would be an easy job. Well, I don't think so now."

"That's why we picked you," Ken shot back.

I couldn't see his expression, of course, but in my mind, I saw the deadpan he assumed when he was trying to be funny.

Our joking soon turned serious. Ken was genuinely as surprised and shocked as all of us had been by the Fed's revelations. But I had learned that it was pretty hard to 'ruffle' Ken. We talked about the next steps. I told him about our plan to engage Ed Herlihy and mentioned that I would like to have Alice Herald work with me. He agreed but stressed the importance of keeping him and the management engaged. After all, they would have to do whatever detailed work was involved. Jeff Lacker had made this same point.

By Monday afternoon, all five of us were meeting with Ed Herlihy and his team at the offices of Wachtell, Lipton, Rosen, and Katz in New York City. Wachtell occupied two or three floors in the stately, thirty-eight story CBS Building, close to Rockefeller Center in the city's midtown. We had access to secretarial assistance, as well as coffee, snacks, restrooms, and break rooms for private conversations and phone calls — all on the same floor. It was a comfortable setting we greatly appreciated.

As we began to get organized, the magnitude of the task before us became glaringly apparent. It turned out, almost serendipitously, that we had an excellent team.

Tom May, a CPA, paid exquisite attention to detail. As chair of the board's Audit Committee, he was very knowledgeable about the bank's controls and risks. And, importantly, he was on good terms with regulators from the Fed and the OCC. Frank Bramble had been through a similar situation at another bank and was able to offer the benefit of his experience. And he had worked with Ed before. I didn't know Charles Rossotti as well as I knew the others, but his hard work and willingness to pitch in wherever needed proved invaluable. Chad Gifford had by now joined us in person. He brought not only a wealth of experience as a seasoned former bank CEO and chairman but also an outsized and offbeat sense of humor that came in handy whenever the pressure of our work threatened to reach boiling point.

Our mood was sober but not grim. We quickly got down to business and assigned various tasks to committee members. Perhaps I should not have been surprised at how quickly I was acknowledged and accepted as the team leader. But I was. One of the most difficult tasks we had was to reconstitute the board, to add more people with banking and finance experience. That meant some people would have to leave. The team was unanimous in its decision that, at the appropriate time, I should be the one to call the board members individually to ask them either to offer their resignation or to agree to remain on the board. This would turn out to be a very wrenching assignment.

Tom and Chad agreed to lead the Management Assessment and Succession Planning effort; Charles and Frank would lead the review of Risk Operations. These were two additional assignments we had. In order to keep the other directors up to date, each of us was assigned specific directors to call on a regular basis. My job also was to keep Ken and his team apprised of our work.

On Tuesday, I arrived in Charlotte directly from New York to meet with Ken and the bank's senior management. I brought them up to date on what our committee had discussed and how we were going to organize ourselves. We talked about the conclusions of the Stress Test, and the press release that had to come from the bank.

After my meeting with Ken and senior management, we held the conference call with the board. By now I was beginning to feel the physical and mental toll of the past week's developments — the shock of being named chairman; the urgent meeting with the feds in Virginia, with its dreadful news and the tremendous responsibility dropped on my shoulders; back-to-back flights from Chicago to Richmond, back to Chicago, and from there to New York and then to Charlotte. Indeed, my shoulders ached. I didn't think my blood pressure was up, despite the slight throbbing in my head. But at all costs, I had to keep my fatigue from Ken and the board. I did not want them to think that I was not physically up to the job of chairman.

I told the board about my call from Kevin Warsh; together, the five of us described our meeting with Jeff Lacker and his colleagues and the proposed agreement with the Fed. We walked them through it, explaining what we thought had to happen. We had a very spirited discussion with lots of questions. Our group had to convey not just the substance of the meeting and documents, but also the tone and gravity of Lacker's comments. They were as surprised as we had been, though, by this time, we'd had a few days to absorb things.

Nevertheless, on the whole, most of the board members were realistic about the situation we faced. We all knew the country was in dire economic circumstances. Debate still raged about whether the Obama administration would nationalize big banks to keep them solvent. A government takeover was a scary proposition. We felt our own bank was very vulnerable. We were still in debt to the Fed for forty-five billion dollars through the Troubled Asset Relief Program as part of the deal we reached with them to cushion the purchase of loss-beleaguered Merrill Lynch. And we also were in debt to them for a $118 billion loss-protection guarantee. The bank and the Fed had identified a package of assets that were risky. The Fed had then given us a guarantee of $118 billion that we could draw on to cover losses if these assets actually went bad. And at $33.9 billion, we had the largest shortfall of the ten banks that needed to raise new capital in order to survive a deeper recession, according to the Tests. Wells Fargo had the second largest, but theirs was much lower than ours, at $13.7 billion. Citigroup had to raise just $5.5 billion, the fourth-largest shortfall.

With our indebtedness to the Fed and our Stress Test shortfall, it was a scary position for Bank of America to be in. The thought of it exacerbated my angst about the press release.

The board was well acquainted with the bank's financial situation. Most of the directors — the great majority, in fact — understood that we had no other option but to agree to the Fed's proposal. The need to reconstitute the board was the most sensitive and delicate part of the discussion. The agreement the board was being asked to sign included the revamping of the board itself! Just imagine. We had to ask the directors to agree to have many of themselves eventually removed, and also agree to appoint a special committee to carry out said removal. In graphic terms, we were asking the board to turn over its power to a special committee composed of the Richmond five — the four people I'd asked to accompany me to Richmond, and me.

In the end, they agreed to have the Richmond five move forward on implementing the agreement and to constitute a Special Committee to act on behalf of the board.

On Wednesday, I was back in New York, working with the staff at Wachtell, Lipton, Rosen, and Katz to get our Special Committee organized. The committee's work that day involved much more than the Stress Test. Indeed, the press release would announce not only the existence of the Special Committee to the world but also our work agenda for the next several months. On Thursday, I would be in Charlotte again for a conference call with the media to take questions about the press release.

At this point, barely a full week had passed since I had been named chairman. And it wasn't as if my life outside of the bank had suddenly come to a halt. I still had obligations to other organizations and companies with which I was affiliated. I had flown to New York on Sunday for Monday's meeting with Ed Herlihy, but I had a 9 a.m. call with a U.S. Tennis Association committee on the same Monday, and a noon call with the McDonald's Audit Committee — all before the 1 p.m. meeting with Ed and the Special Committee. And immediately after my big day with the press release on Thursday, I had to leave for Sewanee: The University of the South, located in the middle of the Smoky Mountains in Tennessee, to receive an honorary degree.

Shirley and I tried to keep up with each other by phone during all of my going-and-coming. She could accompany me on some of my trips to Mellon and the USTA, but the Bank of America meetings were, of course, off-limits.

It would be disingenuous of me, not to say totally untrue, to gloss over the intensity of the pressure I felt in the days leading up to my public debut as chairman of the bank. So much was riding on the content and tone of our Stress Test press release. I confess without shame that I experienced more than one sleepless night in the process of helping to craft that release. The fact that the bank's public relations team was primarily responsible for the work did little to assuage my angst. After all, I would be the one, along with Ken, quoted by name.

I was terribly worried about how the release would come across. Its language had to communicate unequivocally to

139

the government that the bank was serious about carrying out the terms of the agreement laid out in Richmond, without conveying to the public at large that we were under a mandate from the government. To the external audience — the general public, the domestic and international financial community, the media, and politicians spooked by the financial services meltdown, the bank's $45 billion federal 'loan,' and the worst economic recession in seventy years — it had to convey a sense of confidence in the bank's present position. And to the bank's shareholders, it had to show that we were on top of things even though the $33.9 billion capital increase the Federal Reserve said we needed was far greater than what had been called for by any other bank.

Even as I agonized over my language for the press release, I also was very worried about how I would handle myself in front of the press after the release was made public. I had participated in numerous press conferences before, but those were almost always connected to the announcement of good news — a major research grant at the National Science Foundation; the dedication of a new building at Morehouse; a new scientific breakthrough at Argonne. These were low-key occasions compared to what was ahead.

The language of the press release had to relay that the board would be making significant changes, without mentioning that we had an agreement with the bank's regulators. The release would be the first public announcement that the board would be restructured. Although I had reported this to the members on our May 5th call, they and all of their friends, family members, and colleagues would be reading it for the first time in the public media. We certainly did not want any directors to resign prematurely. These people were CEOs, heads of important not-for-profits, a retired four-star general, a retired admiral, and the like — men and women at the zenith of their respective careers. What was to stop any of them from saying, "Well, I'm going to leave right now," if they had read in the newspapers or heard on television that Bank of America said in an official press release that the board was going to be revamped? Why wait for the revamping?

We could not afford to have any directors leave just then. By almost every measure, the banking industry was experiencing one of the worst years in its history, and the business of Bank of America had to continue. We had committees to fill, assignments to be completed, work to be done. Furthermore, a large exodus of directors at this time would have shattered the impression the press release was intended to give — that the bank was on top of things. It would have looked like a purge or a fleeing from a sinking ship, and that could really spook the markets. We needed all of our directors to stay engaged until they were asked to leave.

That was one of the trickiest things we had to do.

For me, getting ready for the press release was far more stressful than having to submit to the Stress Test itself. That was mostly the management's job. On the other hand, I could not get Jeff Lacker's words out of my head, "The eyes of the financial community are going to be on you." The plan was to have our response ready for media distribution on the afternoon of the 6th, for release to the public the following day. The bank's PR team had gone to work as soon as we had given them the government's financial results and the gist of the Richmond meeting. They came up with several drafts, which they sent to Ken and to all of us on the special committee. Copies were sent to Jeff Lacker and also to the Fed, OCC, and the Office of the Secretary of the Treasury, Tim Geithner. Everyone wanted to make sure the 'right' message — at least from their perspective — was conveyed.

I was at home when I got a call from Geithner. I was astonished. I had never met or spoken with Geithner before, and as far as I knew, neither he nor his office had been involved in reviewing the press release up to now. On the phone, Geithner indicated that he was not happy with the draft he had seen. He felt the bank needed to be more specific about its plan for the capital increase. How were we going to raise the $33.9 billion? What were we going to do, exactly?

We also needed stronger and more specific language about the fact that there would be changes in the current board membership, he said. For all the reasons I mentioned earlier, we definitely did not want to do this. I was noncommittal with the Secretary. I didn't push back. I simply listened. But I felt very strongly that I could not accede to his wishes. I reported the conversation to the other committee members, and they unanimously agreed with the position I took.

The phone call lasted only a few minutes. It was the first and only conversation I had with Secretary Geithner. I have no idea how he felt about the final version of our press release. In fact, I never heard from him again.

I had struggled and struggled with the language of the press release referring to board changes, and was still struggling with what precise language to use. On Tuesday, I was restless all night and could not sleep. As sometimes happened when I was wrestling with a difficult physics problem, the answer suddenly came to me. Instead of speaking about the need to 'change an inadequate' board, we should focus on good 'corporate governance' in all respects. And that could include a restructuring of the board. The press release should emphasize that the Bank of America would set an example of good governance and show that the board acted in that regard.

I called Ed Herlihy early the next morning and shared my idea with him.

"How does that sound, Ed?"

Ed responded immediately. "This is wonderful, Walter. This is perfect. You should be the writer."

I then called the bank's PR team and gave them the statement I had come up with. We had a rule: no emails, only phone calls.

The PR team also liked the statement. They captured the language in the following words that were used in the press release: "Massey emphasized that the Bank of America board is committed to being recognized as an exemplar of good corporate governance practices and to listening carefully to shareholder views. "To this end," he continued, "the board has established a committee chaired by me and including four other non-executive directors: Frank P. Bramble Sr., Charles K. Gifford, Thomas J. May, and Charles O. Rossotti. In addition to overseeing Bank of America's response to the Supervisory Capital Assessment Process, the committee is charged with reviewing and recommending changes in all aspects of the board's activities, from the structure and charters of its standing committees, to board meetings and agendas, to board composition and size."

Board composition and size. That was the key ambiguous phrase. Hinting that there would be changes on the board without saying so directly.

CHAPTER TWENTY-ONE
D-DAY

The long-awaited day arrived, Thursday, May 7th, 2009. The government's Stress Test findings and our response were now public. It was time for the new chairman to face reporters.

My own stress level hovered in celestial orbit all day. What questions would I get? The press release indicated that Ken Lewis, Joe Price, and I would discuss the results on a conference call at 6 p.m. But the bank's PR people arranged for me to be available to the press throughout the day, both by phone and in person. When it was time for the 6 p.m. media conference call, I found myself in a room with some of the PR team that had prepped me. Ken and Joe were on separate media calls.

"Okay. Are you ready?" one of the PR staff said to me.

"I'm as ready as I can be," I replied. I showed them my game face.

"Great! We're going to plug in the press."

"All right."

Officious media sounds drifted into the room. Paper rustled. A microphone crackled. Keyboards clicked. A throat cleared.

"We have on the line here, Dr. Walter Massey, chairman of the board. He's willing to take questions. Please identify yourselves before you ask your question," the PR staffer announced.

I do not recall the name of every reporter who plied me with questions, but I am pretty sure Dan Fitzpatrick from *The Wall Street Journal* was on the line. Dan conducted the very first interview with me for the national press. Over the course of my time as chairman, his scoops on what was discussed in our board meetings would be the bane of the board. It was as if he had a microphone or a plant in the room.

I handled the media better than I thought I would. I was pressed for details about changes the board would make, but I only said that we would seek new directors with more banking and financial experience. My remark, "Our model is not broken," must have resonated strongly with the reporters. It frequently appeared in their articles.

On the whole, I thought news reports of Thursday evening's press conferences with Ken, Joe Price, and myself were balanced and fair, even positive. Statements by Ken and Joe were consistent with everything we had discussed. News organizations emphasized the points we hoped they would and conveyed the messages we wanted them to, both in terms of the bank's ability to create the reserve to meet the requirements of the Supervisory Capital Assessment Program, and in terms of our board governance.

In most cases, we were mentioned in a broader report on the government's findings for all nineteen stress-test banks. Analysts weighed in with candid comments about our particular internal situation. They gave their take on what they saw as the true nature of the regulators' post-stress-test recommendations to the banks. Almost every article alluded to the shareholders' meeting in April that resulted in Ken's removal as chairman and my elevation to that position.

In a way, the day was somewhat anti-climactic. Media organizations had gotten hold of the Stress Test results before the government's announcement and had concluded that the sky was not falling. The same day that the government announced the results, *The New York Times* reported, "the verdict was far more upbeat than many in the industry had feared when the tests were first announced in February." Furthermore, the newspaper said, "the banks that came up short will have to raise much less than some analysts had expected as recently as a few days ago ... Industry executives reacted with jubilation as if they had proved their critics wrong and passed the tests with flying colors."

And there was Tim Geithner's upbeat remark to reporters that "This transparent, conservatively-designed test should result in a more efficient, stronger banking system."

None of this mattered to Bank of America's fiercest detractors. Some of their comments were downright brutal.

Anna Burger, the secretary-treasurer of the Service Employees International Union, said the Stress Test results proved "what concerned shareholders, taxpayers, and bank employees have been saying all along — Bank of America is a sinking ship that needs more than just a change in captain to address fundamentally unsustainable and irresponsible business practices that are bad for consumers, bad for employees, and dangerous for our larger economy."

In the press release — and I'm certain in his own encounters with the media — Ken came across as he usually did: very calm and controlled. But I suspect that preparing for the press release took as much of a toll on him as it did on me.

"Never was a test so aptly named," he said to reporters Thursday evening. Those words were widely quoted.

I certainly agree with his assessment. Mentally preparing for the press release to announce our results was the first and one of the most challenging episodes of my new chairmanship. Many others would follow.

Ken's comportment throughout the entire ordeal — from the time I briefed him on the meeting in Richmond to our press conferences — reaffirmed my early impressions of him and what it would be like to work with him. Ken had been Hugh McColl's go-to guy on acquisitions and had successfully overseen expansions in Texas, Florida, and elsewhere. I wasn't that familiar with him when he succeeded Hugh as CEO in

2001. Like Hugh, he seemed buttoned-down and all business. I got to know him better after he became CEO. He was not egotistical or self-centered at all, but extremely ambitious for the bank. I felt that, apart from his family, the bank was his life.

I found Ken an effective, no-nonsense leader — no carbon copy of Hugh McColl. He was certainly decisive in demoting people, and in acquiring other financial institutions. His statements in the press release certainly came across as resolute.

"We are comfortable with our current capital position in the present economic environment," he said. "The stress test asks what if the economy does much worse than most experts project. We are working on a plan to submit to the government for such a contingency, which is due by June 8th. While it would have a number of components, we will not need any new government money. The plan will be implemented by the November 9th deadline. Bank of America will continue to be the leading financial services company for consumers and businesses. We are well-capitalized with the best liquidity of any large bank. We continue to lead the industry in making new loans and to serve our customers and clients with innovative products. We understand our responsibility to our communities, customers, and shareholders."

My own press conference ran for thirty- to forty-five minutes. All in all, I thought the day went pretty well. As well as I might have expected. Ken, Joe, and the PR team felt pretty good about it, too. I didn't celebrate. I couldn't, not knowing what the media would report the next day. But I felt relieved that I had gotten through one of my first hurdles as chairman. I recalled, yet again, Jeff Lacker's warning that the eyes and ears of global banking would hone in on me on this day, and I felt satisfied that I had delivered myself in a manner worthy of my position. I also felt that the PR team, Ken, and his senior management team and I were working together very well, and that made me feel good about what was to come.

For the first time in more than a week, I began to relax. The heaviness in my neck and shoulders eased, which was a good thing for a man with my particular health challenges. I take medication to keep my high blood pressure under control. The week of May 1st to May 7th certainly was one of the most stressful I had ever endured, but I kept myself out of dangerous territory.

Newspapers labeled me a man of "quiet demeanor." They could not have known that I had a recipe for that demeanor. One of the most effective ways that I've learned to control stress is to exercise. I had to make sure that I scheduled some form of exercise into my daily work routine. My secretary and assistants knew that. And so, even in those turbulent days of my new chairmanship, no matter how busy it got, every day I would take time off to play tennis, do Pilates, or find some other way to work out. I can only imagine how that must have seemed to those who were not aware of my health situation. But I heard no snide remarks and saw no side-eyes.

That's not to say that I didn't feel somewhat guilty at times about taking off to play tennis. But I got over that because I realized how important it was to me. You learn to listen to your body.

When I first confided in Alice Herald that I had high blood pressure, I warned her that I needed to control my temper and level of stress. Alice was a trim, fit woman in her 50s, born in southern California. She was outgoing, incredibly efficient, invariably cheerful, and upbeat even in the most trying situations. I trusted her completely and was never disappointed. Obviously, she made it her duty to keep me in check. Sometimes when I got very upset about something, she would caution me cheerily, "Watch your blood pressure, Walter. Don't get upset. Watch your blood pressure."

May 7th, 2009, was history, but there were hurdles yet to be crossed in my chairmanship. I knew what those hurdles were.

Chapter Twenty-Two
A WELCOME BREAK

I flew back to Chicago on a bank plane immediately after the Stress Test press conference. I was already beginning to see how access to a bank plane would make a huge difference in my performance of the job of chairman. Obviously, there were rules governing my use of the plane. Steele and I had gone over this and other job-related matters, such as office space, expense reporting, and travel in general, soon after I became chairman.

"Walter, you will be able to use a bank plane for all your official travel. Just coordinate with Nancy Dry. Give her your schedule. However, I want to warn you never to do any personal travel," he told me, then added with a smile, "No matter how much you might be tempted to invite Shirley along on a trip, don't do it, because it will cost you an awful amount of money."

I smiled back and quipped, "Don't worry. But can I send pictures?"

Shirley never accompanied me on the company plane, but, on occasion, others who had nothing to do with the bank did. One such trip stands out. It came later that summer when Nancy called me with a request the day before one of my trips from Chicago to New York.

"Walter, do you mind if there are some extra passengers on the plane with you tomorrow?"

"Of course not," I replied.

When I boarded the plane the next morning, I expected to see some of the senior bank officers, who often flew along with me for their own business. Instead, a family of four — father, mother, and two small children (a boy and a girl) — boarded after I had seated myself. Very politely, almost meekly, the father said, "Good morning, sir. Thank you so much for this. It really means a lot."

The family was Caucasian. The father, middle-aged, was definitely not dressed like a banker. I had no idea what he was thanking me for. The pilot educated me later.

It turned out that the bank often offered free transportation to medical patients when there was room on the plane. The little boy was going to New York for surgery.

The weirdest feeling came over me then. Here was this white family offering me thanks for the ride as though it were my plane. I couldn't help thinking what a long way this was from Mississippi. "What would all those white people I grew up with think of this?" The question filled my mind for several moments, and then I thought what a wonderful thing it was for the bank to do! I was deeply moved by the episode. I felt proud of the bank and proud that I was so intimately associated with it.

My flight from Charlotte followed the Stress Test press conference, and I didn't arrive in Chicago until almost eleven o'clock that night. Shirley was still up when I got home. This was unusual. She normally went to bed very early when I was away and would call to give me notice before she turned in: "I am going to bed now, so don't call later. Love you."

To this, I would reply, "*What?* It's only nine o'clock."

This was our routine. But when I arrived home that night, she was full of questions.

"How did it go? What did they ask you?"

I said I thought it went very well, but we'd see what the papers said tomorrow. I was tired, and we had to travel to Sewanee the following day. I hadn't even packed.

I awoke with a good feeling on that Friday, May 8th. I'd slept better than I had since before my trip to Richmond. Jeff Lacker had emphasized that the entire financial community would be watching me, and I felt that I had not disappointed them. Newspapers reported Wall Street had favorable reactions to the remarks Ken, Joe Price, and I had made about the Stress Test results.

"The fact that BofA came out yesterday and said this is how we are going to do it, 'A, B, and C,' got them a lot of fans," research analyst Nancy Bush said in an Associated Press report that several newspapers picked up.

The real work of the Special Committee had to begin immediately. We had met only once so far, and I could feel the pressure starting to build. We had to settle into the business of making good on our agreement with the feds. The committee was scheduled to meet again in New York that Monday, May 11th, to map out our work plan.

I called Jeff before I left for Sewanee, The University of the South in Tennessee. A lot had been riding on the press conference, and Jeff had played an important role leading up to it. I was sure he had followed it closely, and I wanted his opinion of how it went.

"Jeff, it's Walter. I assume you read about the press conference."

"Hi, Walter. Yes, I did." He sounded pretty cheerful, not at all as serious as he was in Richmond.

"What did you think of it?" I tried to sound cool.

"I thought it went well, Walter. You sent the right signals to the right people," he assured me.

"Thanks, Jeff. I'm glad to hear that."

His assurance heightened my good feeling, and I departed for Tennessee.

Sewanee, as the university is popularly called, is a fascinating place. One of the country's oldest colleges, it was established in 1857. It is a private, Episcopalian school, nestled in the mountains overlooking the Tennessee Valley. It sits on 13,000 acres of forests, bluffs, meadows, lakes, and caves, rendering it one of the most beautiful campuses in the country. Like nearly all our nation's colleges, its history ties it to slavery. Sewanee is closely linked to the Confederacy and aristocratic traditions of the South as well as to the Church of England, and the academic models set by Oxford and Cambridge. Union soldiers blew up its cornerstone during the Civil War. Construction resumed after the war, with financial support from the Church of England.

I always have mixed feelings when I visit these old southern institutions. I realize they have changed, but there is still a lingering feeling of — what? Certainly, pride at being honored, but something else, too. Distrust? Resentment? Guilt for being there? I'm not quite sure. I suppose I feel a little of each.

Shirley and I flew — on a commercial flight, of course — to Nashville, where two young men, Clayton and Tim, met us for the hour-and-a-half drive to the campus. It was a delightful drive through mountains and lush valleys, and I felt myself beginning to relax. I enjoyed the conversation with Clayton and Tim, who were both students at the university and clearly loved the school.

The ceremony I participated in closely modeled that of English colleges. The centuries-old rituals of the Commencement amplified the breathtaking beauty of the campus.

I like rituals and ceremonies, especially when they reflect on history and tradition. I believe they can be very important in reinforcing a sense of community and cohesiveness in an institution. At Morehouse, first as a student and then as president, I loved participating in our ceremonies, steeped as they were in black history and civil rights. Given Sewanee's history, it was somewhat surprising, and gratifying, to see African-American faculty, staff, students, and alumni participating in the commencement formalities.

My spirits soared as the ceremony got underway in the All Saints Chapel, which was built in 1890. The chapel's exquisite beauty reminded me of Westminster Abbey in London. Wandering about the picturesque campus with Shirley after it was over, I felt utterly relaxed.

This was the very first public occasion I attended since being named chairman. My ascent to chairmanship occurred so recently that it was not even mentioned in the Honorary Degree Citation, as that had been printed well in advance of Commencement. However, at the dinner that evening, I was introduced as the new Chairman of Bank of America, and that elicited great applause. Several guests were from the financial industry and wanted to talk. I had very engaging conversations with them, all the while thinking, "This is for real. I am the new chairman of Bank of America."

The weekend at Sewanee was a welcome break from the demands of my new position. Thus, it was with a sense of renewed energy that I went into the Special Committee meeting in New York the following Monday.

Chapter Twenty-Three
SOLDIERING ON

The work plan we mapped out that Monday was now in place. Between May and October, our group made substantial progress on all of our goals. We relied on detailed work, and support from the bank's management and staff, as well as from certain outside experts. We kept Ken informed of everything we did.

The urgency of our work weighed on us, but we never felt panicked. Our meetings typically were somber affairs with rare instances of levity. Everyone was very cooperative, and the meetings ran smoothly and efficiently. The mix of individuals present ensured that they did.

Special Committee meetings were held in New York City, or in Charlotte at the bank's headquarters. Our New York venue was a large conference room at the offices of Wachtell, Lipton, Rosen & Katz, where we had the benefit of Ed Herlihy and his colleagues. Ed was very good at pointing out questions he thought we should be asking ourselves while recognizing that he was there as a legal and strategic consultant, and not to run the meeting. He never tried to do so, anyway. His partner, Larry Makow, was also a valuable member of our team. Larry was the guy who kept us on track, always reminding us, in a pleasant but insistent manner, of the tasks we had to complete and the schedules we had to keep. He and Ed were an excellent team.

Fortunately, we did not have to guess what we had to do, which made it fairly easy to divide the work among our team. We had to work on management succession planning, assessment of our risk operations, replacement of the board, and how we were going to raise the capital that was required through the Stress Test. Sometimes, when a group is faced with such a formidable task as we were, they may be unsure of where to start, or how to prioritize the work involved. Our group had the advantage of knowing what we had to do, and by when we had to accomplish it.

The question arose as to how to go about finding new board members. It didn't take us long to come up with a process.

"We could hire a search firm."

"That means we'd have to interview a number of them, and we don't have time for that."

"Right. We're better off doing it ourselves. We know what we're looking for, and we know people who might fit the bill."

"We could also bring in consultants to help us."

"And Ed and Ken. They would be a great help."

"That settles it. We do it ourselves, get a few consultants to work with us, and reach out to Ed and Ken as well."

Up to that point, the only external insights we had received about the bank's condition had come from our meeting with the Fed in Richmond. So, before we got into the meat of our work, we wanted to get a better sense of how the bank was seen throughout the regulatory community — at the Washington level of the Fed, the OCC, and the FDIC — and throughout the major shareholder community, including the larger investment firms and pension funds.

We brought in a number of knowledgeable people to help with the assessment. Two of them were particularly helpful. One was Eugene "Gene" Ludwig, a former Washington attorney and U.S. Comptroller of the Currency. Gene ran his own consulting firm, Promontory Financial Group when we brought him on. He was well regarded by the Fed in the areas of banking regulation and risk management.

The other extremely helpful consultant was Kendrick 'Ken' Wilson III, who, like Gene, was well respected in financial circles. His college classmates nicknamed him 'Wildcat' because of his 'rough-and-tumble' ways. Hank Paulson hired him as an adviser to the Treasury Department. By then, he had served as vice chairman of investment banking at Goldman Sachs, and in a similar role at Lazard Frères.

"He knows as many people in the whole financial services industry in the U.S. and the world as anybody," Paulson said of him. "Ken was the calm center in the storm of the crisis. I trust his judgment."

Gene and Ken gave us first-rate guidance on what regulators and shareholders identified as the key issues for the bank, and which of those issues they felt we needed to concentrate on. On the whole, all of the consultants we engaged reinforced the fact that we needed more directors with banking experience. After reviewing the material the Fed had given us, they told us that the meeting in Richmond was clearly intended to set a 'tough tone' because the regulators felt that we needed to 'get it.'

We began to collect names of potential board members and pored over our list for a week or so. In a phone meeting at the end of that week, we whittled down the list to between eight and ten people. We wanted to get to around four or five.

In addition to finding new board members, the Committee also had to determine who among the existing directors would be asked to remain on the board. Some of the directors had already informed me that they would be willing to retire from the board if asked, which made this task a little easier.

It was very important that there be no miscommunications between our committee and directors, bank management, and government regulators. It was especially important to keep the other directors in the loop since they still had fiduciary responsibilities and took their duties seriously. We divided the board among ourselves with the understanding that we would regularly call the board members to whom we were assigned to make sure they were kept abreast of our work. My role, among others, was to make sure that Ken Lewis was kept up-to-date.

Richard 'Dick' Parsons, who was chairman of Citigroup at the time, had given me similar advice about keeping the directors in the loop. I'd known Dick for some time, and we had a good relationship. The last time I'd seen him was at Morehouse when he came to speak to a group of students prior to my becoming chair of the bank. We practically shared the same birthday, his being April 4th and mine April 5th. Not that this mattered in the broad scope of what we both were navigating. I simply felt I could trust my instincts about Dick.

I found it intriguing that, in the middle of the worst financial crisis since the Great Depression, the chairmen of two of the largest banks in the country were African American. In normal times, that might have been rich grist for the media mill. Consider, too, that the president of the United States at the same time also was African American. All three of us — Dick, President Obama, and I — had taken up our respective office early in 2009. What would have seemed highly implausible a year before, was now a very real situation in which three Black men were essentially and intimately engaged in steering the financial system of the most powerful country on earth out of a major crisis.

But as far as I can recall, there were no major stories that focused on these particular facts. I am sure the financial media were so concerned about the bigger issue of the day that they had no time for, or interest in, a story that may have appeared to be little more than a human-interest sidebar.

Be that as it may, Dick was one of the first people I called after I became chairman. I didn't call him that very day. I called him a few weeks after I was in the job, after the meeting in Richmond that upended my every expectation of the role I had just assumed. First, he congratulated me on being elevated to chairman. Then he talked about how he was faring at Citi. I recall him emphasizing that he regularly met with the CEO.

"You should meet regularly with the CEO, Walter. You don't want to get too deep into trying to micromanage, but you really need to know at a high level what's going on," he told me. "You need to meet with the CFO, the general counsel, and the board secretary. Make sure you're on top of the thing. Make sure you keep your directors informed."

I appreciated Dick's advice. He had been thrust into the eye of the financial storm as I now was. He became chairman of Citigroup in January when that bank seemed on the brink of collapse — mired in losses, facing lawsuits by irate shareholders, and under scrutiny by regulators and the Justice Department. It was Dick's job to pull it back from the brink, and that he did. He certainly had enough experience to rely on. As head of Dime Savings and Loan Bancorp, he averted disaster during the savings and loan crisis of the 1980s, and he did it with no previous banking experience. His words, when he was named chairman and CEO of Citi, could have come from my own mouth.

"One of my top priorities will be to ensure the Board remains committed to strong, independent, corporate governance — especially in today's challenging economic conditions. I will also work to reconstitute the Board as directors retire, with new members who bring strong, proven business judgment and financial and banking sector expertise," he said.

This certainly resonated strongly with me.

Frequent communication with our immediate stakeholders became a matter of paramount importance. The Special Committee discharged its tasks with laser focus and at a pace that I still contemplate with awe. We met at least twice a week, either by phone or in person. I spent a huge amount of time on the phone because, as usual, I avoided discussing sensitive issues by e-mail. After each meeting of the committee, I would call Lisa and Jennifer at the Fed, Grace at the OCC, and Ken at the bank. I often called Jeff Lacker at the Richmond Fed as well. And as we had planned, regular phone meetings with the rest of the board kept them up-to-date, too.

Actually, 'regular' is an understatement. Whereas the full board typically met five or six times a year, it sometimes met as many as five times a month as the Special Committee proceeded with its work. Between May and December alone, we met with the rest of the board twenty-seven times to keep them abreast of our progress. All but six of those meetings were by phone. We met twice each month in May, June, and September; three times each month in July and August, five times in October and again in December; and four times in November.

Throughout that entire year, the Fed made it clear that they wanted to be kept informed of our progress. But on numerous occasions, they pointed out that it was not their job to tell us how to do things. Our relationship may seem odd in that regard, but it worked well for both of us. I briefed them on where the Committee stood, and what we were thinking, and they told me how that sounded — whether or not we seemed to be on the right track. Then I took that feedback back to the Committee. Never did the Fed say to me, "We don't like that," or "You should do this." They were not in the business of giving detailed orders, which was quite appropriate, and also good for us.

In addition to keeping Ken informed, I stayed in contact with Jeff, Lisa, Jennifer, and Grace. They were very helpful as a sounding board, and in giving the feedback, I needed to pass on to the Committee. Odd as it may seem, I considered them members of our team. Jeff was fine with that. "We all have the same goal to make the bank as healthy as it can be so that the national financial system can be as healthy as it can be," he said.

At no time did I feel that the regulators were breathing down our neck, even though we were constantly in their sights. On the contrary, my open communication with them provided a level of comfort for what we were doing. And beyond giving me honest, straightforward commentary, Jennifer, Grace, and Lisa met periodically with the full board to bring us all up to date on how the agencies saw the Committee's work.

I enjoyed working with these three women. They were appropriately critical, pushy when necessary, always professional, and yet very supportive. They were different from each other in many ways but remarkably similar in others. All three were in their mid-thirties, I guessed, and all three were down-to-earth in a quintessential 'Midwestern' way. They reminded me of many of the young people I had gotten to know when I was the director of the National Science Foundation. They were little known, and in my view, underappreciated individuals who worked in all-important agencies to keep the nation's wheels turning. Dedicated and hardworking, they, and people like them, truly are the backbone of our government.

I teased Grace sometimes. Whenever she called or answered the phone, she would say, 'Hi! This is Grace from the OCC." So, at meetings, I greeted her the same way: 'Hi, Grace from the OCC," to which she usually responded with a smile or chuckle.

As the Committee moved forward, I came to know more intimately and to thoroughly appreciate the personality and expertise of each of my colleagues. I got to know Chad Gifford better than the others because Shirley and I spent time with him and his wife, Ann ("my beautiful wife Ann," as Chad always referred to her), on Nantucket, across the Sound from our place on Cape Cod.

As a former chairman and CEO of Fleet Bank and of Bank of Boston, Chad was the most experienced banker on our Special Committee. In addition to being a director, he was chairman emeritus of Bank of America, which caused us to jokingly refer to each other outside of meetings as "Mr. Chairman."

"How's it going, Mr. Chairman?"

"Fine. And you, Mr. Chairman?"

Chad was the son of a banker. He studied history at Princeton. His mother was a member of the Brown family that founded Brown University, which fascinated me because I had spent so many years at that institution as a faculty member, dean, and trustee. I loved the place. But Chad didn't like to talk about his family's connection to it. When I persisted, he would say, "Oh, so what! That doesn't mean anything."

Chad was a large guy with a face that exhibited honesty and sincerity. He could have been a rugby player. He loved to read, which he did voraciously and on a wide range of subjects. Once, when just the two of us were on a very long flight to recruit a new board member, he looked up from his Kindle and said, "You know Walter, I don't know what I would do if I couldn't read. It would be horrible!" Then he smiled and went back to reading.

Sometimes when he disagreed with Tom May, his old friend, he would wad up paper into a ball and toss it across the table at him, shouting, "Well, that can't be right, Tom." Tom would throw the paper ball right back while the rest of us looked on bewildered. Those were rare moments that relieved the tension during our meetings.

As mentioned earlier, Tom was a meticulous note-taker. He kept us on track and focused. His accounting background showed in the detailed way he approached tasks, but by no means was he the stereotypical dry, humorless CPA. He could be very witty and was a foil for Chad's unorthodox antics. As chair of the Audit Committee, he regularly interacted with the Fed and OCC regulators, and they trusted him. They considered him reliable and a straight shooter. All of this was of immense value to our Committee's work. Tom was willing to take on some of the most onerous and delicate assignments, in particular leading, along with Chad, the assessment of the bank's senior management team, and developing a management succession plan, two of our assignments from the Fed.

I learned that Chad was called "Cha Cha" in college, and I would kid him by calling him that in meetings. He took it in stride and even seemed to enjoy it. His wisdom, experience, and drive were vital to the work of our committee. In meetings and discussions, he could have pulled rank and showed off his experience and banking knowledge compared to mine, but he never did. In formal and informal ways, he always acknowledged that I was the Chairman of the bank and of the Special Committee. In fact, all of the committee members did, which, in retrospect, was remarkable.

Although all of the bank's directors were accomplished, intelligent, and engaged, we needed to bring more banking expertise to the board. That meant asking some of the directors to resign. I was the chairman, so, with the consensus of my colleagues, I took on the job of speaking with most of the directors and asking them to either remain or step down. I felt very apprehensive about doing this. I'd worked with many of these people for years. I trusted and respected them, and some had become my good friends. They had just elected me unanimously to be their Chairman, and now I had to ask some of them to leave.

As painful and distressing as it was for me to ask a departing director to continue doing his or her necessary board work — serving on committees and so forth — even though they knew their job would soon end, it was also a heartening experience. Practically every director with whom I spoke was extremely cooperative and wanted to do what was best for the bank. I was both diplomatic and direct in my approach to them.

I would say, "As you know, we have to restructure the board, and I am calling to thank you for being so cooperative in this process. But, pretty soon, it would be good to have your resignation. Not right now. We need to time things carefully."

A typical response was, "Walter, I know you have to do this. Just let me know when you need my letter of resignation."

But the conversations didn't always go that smoothly. One director was quite angry. Not with me, although he did not hold me blameless.

"We shouldn't let the government push us around! You should have pushed back on all this interfering, Walter," the director snapped.

I simply listened. I saw no point in debating the matter because there was nothing he could do or say to prevent the inevitable. Reluctantly, he decided to cooperate, but he remained explicitly upset. He resigned when he was asked.

My conversation with Jackie Ward, the former head of a telecommunications software company, was one of the most gratifying. She lived in Atlanta, so we would often travel together to board meetings on the company plane. She had her own plane, and a couple of times, we used hers, which was much more richly outfitted than the corporate jets. She was and still is a remarkable person. Born in Milledgeville, Georgia, she still had a deep Southern drawl that belied her sophisticated worldliness. We often talked about family during our flights. I knew that the friendliness I felt towards her was mutual.

Jackie reached out to me early in the restructuring process.

"Walter, I understand what has to be done, and I want to do what would be most helpful," she said. "If you want me to, I will leave immediately, but if you want me to stay, I will. I'm prepared to work in whatever way you think will be most useful."

"Jackie, I really appreciate this and all the advice you've given me in the past," I said.

Her sanguine response to this harrowing task helped me to approach other directors with less angst. A couple of other directors also contacted me and conveyed that, no matter what their fate on the board was, they had been thinking of leaving and wanted to leave. But they would only leave when I thought it was most appropriate.

My discomfort subsided even more.

Ultimately it all worked out better than I could have hoped. By the tenth of June, five directors had resigned. The bank disclosed their departures in its securities filings, stipulating, "Each director's decision to resign was not as a result of any disagreement with the Corporation or its management." The five included Temple Sloan, who had announced my recommendation as chairman at the April 29th board meeting. He resigned on May 26th. Patricia Mitchell, president and CEO of the Paley Center for Media in New York, and Jackie, both resigned on June 8th. Pat joined the board in 2001, the same year Ken became CEO. Jackie joined the NationsBank board in 1994, before the merger with BankAmerica.

In the week that Pat and Jackie resigned, we added four outside directors with experience in banking or financial oversight. The four were Susan S. Bies, a former governor of the Federal Reserve Board and former chief financial officer of First Tennessee National Corp.; William P. Boardman, a retired executive of Bank One Corp. and Visa International Inc.; Donald E. Powell, former chairman of the Federal Deposit Insurance Corp. and former president and chief executive of First National Bank of Amarillo, Texas; and D. Paul Jones, former chairman and CEO of Compass Bancshares Inc.

I was relieved that the job of identifying and recruiting new directors went so smoothly. Still, it was a complex, sensitive undertaking. We needed to keep the process confidential, so we had to be careful how we spoke about the bank's agreement with the Fed. But we also had to be open and honest with the candidates we approached. I called some prospects, and others initially were called by members of the committee who had some previous relationship with them.

When I contacted prospective candidates by phone, I would open with a statement like, "Hi, Bill. Walter Massey here. You may have heard that I am the new chairman of the Bank of America board, and you may also have read that we are going to be making some changes on the board. A colleague and I would like to meet you to see if we might interest you in joining the board."

Responses varied. An initially noncommittal candidate would say something vague like, "Yes, Walter, I've heard about you. Congratulations, by the way. And yes, I've read a little about possible changes on the board."

An outright decline was, "This is quite an honor, but I am really overwhelmed right now." A candidate who was a CEO said, "I don't think my board would approve of my taking on something else now."

Those who wanted to meet promptly declared, "Sure. I'd be happy to talk with you." And I replied to them with, "Great! Let's arrange a meeting. But I must inform you that our conversation has to be kept absolutely confidential since I will be disclosing details of the bank's issues and concerns, including our agreement with the Fed."

All of our prospects were highly experienced professionals. Most were in finance or banking. Some had even been in similar circumstances with regulators or had been regulators themselves. The need for confidential discussions, therefore, did not prove to be a major barrier to recruitment. What candidates were most concerned about were the exact role, authority, and lifespan, of the Special Committee, and how we felt about Ken and his team.

No one spoke disparagingly of the bank. Despite all of the issues for which it was publicly castigated — the Merrill Lynch acquisition, shareholder lawsuits, the Stress Test results — the bank had not lost its prestige and importance. Being a member of our board, therefore, was still an alluring prospect. Consequently, we were able to recruit extremely talented, experienced individuals.

In retrospect, we accomplished this in an astonishingly short period of time — exactly one month, and four days after Chad Gifford, Tom May, Frank Bramble, Charles Rossotti, and I met with the Federal Reserve in Richmond.

CHAPTER TWENTY-FOUR

THE WALL STREET JOURNAL CALLS

A few weeks after the Stress Test press conference, well after the Special Committee had begun its work, *The Wall Street Journal* contacted the bank to set up an interview with me. By then, I had full staff support from the bank, including a communications team. The team told me about the newspaper's request, emphasizing that they really wanted me to do the interview because it could be very good for the bank and for me.

Years later, Dan Fitzpatrick, the reporter who requested and conducted the interview, told me that the bank, at first, would not grant his request. We spoke when I called to tell him that I was writing my memoir and was including a section on his first interview with me.

"The bank was very reluctant," he informed me.

I was surprised. "I thought we were all for it. That's the impression I got when they told me about it."

"Not at first. I spoke with Jim Mahoney to convince the bank to allow me to interview you," he recalled. "I even called Kent Matlock to get him to talk to you."

Jim Mahoney was the head of global corporate communications and public policy at the bank. Kent Matlock was a friend and colleague of mine from Atlanta. He graduated from Morehouse and went on to establish Matlock Advertising, a successful multicultural communications agency in Atlanta. Dan was based in Atlanta at the time of the interview. I can't remember if Kent contacted me on his behalf.

I was nervous about being interviewed by *The Wall Street Journal*, but I felt it was an interview I needed to do. I was now chairman of the bank, and I would have to get used to this kind of thing. But for this particular interview, I thought the timing and logistics might pose a problem. I was on Cape Cod and did not want to travel "off Cape," as Cape Codders say.

"When were they thinking of doing the interview?" I asked. "You know that I'm going to be on Cape Cod for the entire summer."

"Let's see what they say."

Shirley and I have spent our summers on Cape Cod since 1976. We bought our first house there when we were at Brown, and I was Dean of the College. The first time we went to the Cape, we were shocked to see black policemen in the streets. "My God! I didn't know there were Blacks on Cape Cod," I remember exclaiming and Shirley vigorously nodding her head in agreement as we stared at the policemen. It turned out they were Cape Verdeans.

According to some historians, Cape Verdeans first arrived in the United States, and particularly in Cape Cod as highly valued crewmen aboard New England whaling ships in the early nineteenth century. They were picked up from Cape Verde, an archipelago in the Atlantic Ocean, off the western coast of Africa. From this location near Senegal, they eventually settled in the whaling capital of New Bedford, Massachusetts, and in Providence, Rhode Island. Their communities grew exponentially and branched out in the twentieth century as new immigrants arrived. Cape Verdeans were not considered African-Americans. They were brown or dark-skinned, but U.S. authorities officially classified them as "white" or Portuguese. A Cape Verdean friend told me that "white" was even written on their driving licenses for a long time.

Cape Verdeans still celebrate their distinct culture today, but they are far more integrated into the wider African-American community than they'd been in the past. Shirley and I have many Cape Verdean friends today.

After our first visit, Shirley and I got to know Cape Cod quite well from visiting many of our black friends who owned places there or on Martha's Vineyard, the island just off the Cape. We grew to like the area, so we began to look around for a place of our own. As luck would have it, Alice Morse, the wife of Bob Morse, a colleague from Brown, happened to be a real estate agent on the Cape. Bob was a physicist like me and, at one time, had also been Dean of the College at Brown. He and Alice had now 'retired' to the Cape themselves, where Bob worked at WHOI, the Woods Hole Oceanographic Institute, and we had visited them occasionally.

Alice showed us several places, but we could not afford any of the ones we really liked. I had almost given up on the idea of buying on the Cape when Shirley went there with Alice one day to see yet another prospect.

She called me about three that afternoon. I was in my office at Brown.

"Walter, you have to come down now and see this place!"

"Do I have to? Are you sure about this place?" I replied a bit peevishly. "You know I'm really busy right now."

Shirley was insistent. "Yes, I think you ought to see it."

"Okay! Okay!" I gave in reluctantly, figuring we could always have a nice dinner on the Cape if the viewing didn't work out.

Back then, traffic was not as heavy as it is today, so at that time of day, it took only about forty-five minutes to drive to the Cape from Brown. The place Alice showed us was a charming old farmhouse on a fairly large piece of property, right across the street from the Great Sippewissett Marsh and Buzzard's Bay. That meant we could walk to the beach and go clamming and fishing. The property even had a white picket fence.

After I looked around, I said to Alice, "This is wonderful, Alice, but you know it's out of our price range." I had checked the listing.

"I know Walter, but the Doutharts would like you two to own the place. They're willing to drop the price considerably."

The Doutharts were a white family, and the property had been in their family for generations, but they had decided to live elsewhere.

"How much?" I said.

I couldn't believe the figure Alice quoted. "*What!* Really? Are you sure?" I managed.

"Yes. Definitely," Alice said with a firm nod.

"We'll take it. But do you know why they're willing to do this?" I said.

"Their daughter is a student at Brown. She told her parents that as Dean, you had been very helpful to her and to many other students. She encouraged them to sell their home to you and your family."

Well, my goodness! Aloud, I said, "Wow, that's just great!"

Honestly, I did not remember the young lady. But it proved once again that the way you treat others affects you later in life. As an old saying goes, "Your deeds travel with you from afar."

I got another surprise when I told one of my colleagues at Brown that we had purchased in the West Falmouth Village Historic District on the Cape. Yetta Glicksman, the wife of the provost, Maurice, who is Jewish, said, "*What!* They don't even sell to Jews there!"

I had no idea if that was true. But we probably were the first black family that was not Cape Verdean to buy in that specific area. We loved it and still do. We've never encountered overt racism, perhaps because we lived in a very special world as mostly 'summer people.' We later moved to Sippewissett, not far from where we were before, but still on Buzzard's Bay. People often ask us what we do there all summer. "We live there," I would say. We're not 'on vacation' when we're on Cape Cod. We simply change residences.

I still work when we're there, using the phone and the Internet. I also travel for business and attend lectures at the Marine Biological Laboratory and the Woods Hole Oceanographic, two local institutions. But it is a much more relaxed setting, and there is more time for tennis, going to the beach, and visiting friends on Nantucket and Martha's Vineyard.

I felt I needed the balm of Cape Cod more than ever that summer of 2009.

The Wall Street Journal offered to send Dan Fitzpatrick to Cape Cod for the interview. The bank's communications team swung into action, briefing me on questions I might be asked.

After the ordeal of the Stress Test press release and press conference, preparing for this interview might have seemed like a cakewalk. Nothing could be further from the truth. This would be a live, face-to-face interview with what was sure to be a top-notch reporter. Jim Mahoney would be the only bank representative in the room. I would not simply be announcing the results of the Stress Test and answering related questions from multiple news organizations. Rather, this would be an interview about who I was, what I brought to the job of chairman of the board of Bank of America, and my goals for my tenure. It would be published in a newspaper of national and international reach.

Local and regional publications had carried stories about me after I was named chairman, but those were usually just summaries of my official bio. A typical example was *Charlotte Business Journal*'s article, "A Look at Walter Massey, BofA's New Chairman," published April 30th. No one from the publication had interviewed me for that piece.

The Special Committee had been working for about a month by the time *The Wall Street Journal* requested an interview, so we expected Dan to ask about what we had been doing. The bank had already announced the appointment of new board members and Dan had published an article about them on the fifth of June, titled, "BofA Gets New Blood for Board."

I was not known to *The Wall Street Journal,* or to the public at large when I became chairman, so I wanted to project gravitas and knowledge. I wanted to make sure I got the tone right, and that I answered the questions correctly without giving away inappropriate information. I was deeply concerned about the signals I would send to shareholders, and to the bank associates, including senior management, and all three-hundred-thousand or so people who worked for the bank.

Understandably, morale at the bank was not great, given all the uncertainty about whether we were going to be nationalized. In addition to the scary financial issues, management and associates were faced with changes at the very top, i.e., a new chairman and a major 'restructuring' of the board. A conversation I had with Joe Price around that time came to mind.

"Walter," Joe said, "the team hasn't had a break since January. People are worn out."

"I know, Joe, and it's good that you bring it up as we begin to move through these issues. Please let everyone know how much we appreciate their hard work."

I was concerned about the situation Joe described, but, as a non-executive chairman, there was only so much I could do. One thing I *could* do, however, was signal that at the board level, we were doing our job to help guide the bank through these troubled times.

So I wanted to make sure everyone took away from my interview the right feelings about me as their new chairman, and that, under my chairmanship in this time of crisis, the board was steadfast in ensuring that the right people were put in place to effectively manage the bank's operations.

I felt as anxious as I had in 1999 when I was the brand-new director of the National Science Foundation and had to testify before Congress on the foundation's budget submission. On that occasion, I believed that my bearing — my entire demeanor, for that matter — had to inspire confidence in me as the foundation's head. I wanted the NSF staff, the broader scientific community, and the senators on the Appropriations

Sub-committee to feel that the decision to make me the director was the right decision. I tried to talk down my anxiety, telling myself that I had a prepared script, that I'd been thoroughly drilled on questions I might be asked, and that I would be speaking to a largely supportive audience. After all, I was nominated by President George H. W. Bush and unanimously confirmed in the Senate. But I couldn't get rid of my nervousness about having to send the right signals.

All I knew about Dan Fitzpatrick before we met was that he was widely read and very influential in the financial community. I had no idea what he looked like or what kind of interviewer he was. The bank told him how to contact me, and he called me before our interview to find out where we would meet.

"I'm on the board of the Marine Biological Laboratory, a major research lab here on Cape Cod. We could meet there. They may let us use the conference room. I'll check with them," I told him.

Aside from MBL — that's how everyone referred to the Marine Biological Lab — and the Woods Hole Oceanographic Institution, the Woods Hole Research Center, the Woods Hole Science Aquarium, the National Oceanic, and Atmospheric Administration's Northeast Fisheries Science Center, and a U.S. Geological Survey Coastal and Marine Science Center were also nearby.

MBL gladly agreed to our using their venue. On Saturday, June 6, the day of the interview, I drove from our home in Falmouth to Woods Hole about fifteen minutes away. It's a pleasant drive. This part of the Cape is green and forested, unlike the outer Cape with its picturesque, postcard-gracing dunes. The trees lend a quietness and tranquility that I love. Coupled with the distinctive fishy, briny smell of ocean air, it is a wonderful place to be.

I met Dan and his photographer, along with Jim Mahoney, at the entrance to the Candle House, a historic facility on the waterfront in Woods Hole that commemorates the area's nineteenth-century whaling industry. Candle House was built at the height of that industry. It was so named because it served as a warehouse for whale oil, some of which was made into candles. MBL bought the land and the building in 1903 and made it the home of its administrative offices and classrooms. A recently restored replica of the prow of an 1840s whaling ship juts out from the building's original stone façade.

The interview took place in one of their conference rooms. Since it was a Saturday, there were only a few people around — those who normally worked throughout the entire weekend and the campus manager, who was there to accompany us.

We heard a few excited whispers as we made our way to the conference room. It was not often that *The Wall Street Journal* came for an interview. Science journals, yes. *The Wall Street Journal*, hardly.

"You're a celebrity," I said to Dan.

"I thought all the fuss was about you," he replied, smiling.

The conference room was designed to resemble the interior of a sailing ship. It was not fancy at all, exhibiting the sparseness typical of research institutions. There were small offices around the perimeter of the room. A large table sat in the center. Bulletin boards carried notices of scientific talks and marine excursions. Dan's photographer had me pose for a picture in front of the large oval window that overlooked the bay. The same picture accompanied Dan's original article on our interview.

Dan was a fairly young, good-looking man with a boyish smile. Genial. Not stuffy at all. I liked him almost immediately.

"Wow! This place is the perfect setting. So different from the usual office interview," he said. "It's really nice to be able to come to Cape Cod for the weekend."

It was not going to be all work for him. That's probably why the interview was more relaxed than I had anticipated. It lasted for about an hour. Dan was direct and asked probing questions, but it was not a 'gotcha' exchange where he tried to entrap me into revealing information about the bank that could compromise my integrity.

"You were very cautious, but you didn't try to manipulate the conversation. You chose your words carefully," Dan recalled when we spoke years later.

He was right. I always try to choose my words carefully, but I was particularly mindful of doing so then.

I got to know Dan very well after that first interview. He was a remarkably good reporter — friendly, chatty, and above all, persistent. I gave him my cell number, and he would call me directly. Actually, he called more often than I cared for. A call from him usually began with, "Walter, I just want to try this out on you now. This is what I'm hearing."

He would then launch into whatever it was that he was hearing and end with, "What do you think? It doesn't have to be for the record."

I would reply, "Dan, I just can't comment at all."

He was exceptional at getting information. Even after I stepped down as chairman, he would call me to ask about the bank or about other activities I was engaged in. This lasted for years.

"I remember those telephone exchanges well. I always respected the way you handled yourself. You never dismissed me, even though you had no intention of giving me the information I wanted. You stayed true to the bank. I admired you for that," he confided when I told him I was writing my memoir.

That first interview was published the following Monday, June 8th, with the headline, "Massey, a Physicist, Re-Engineers BofA." It pulled no punches. As it turned out, I needn't have worried about revealing the details of the meeting in Richmond with the Fed. Dan seemed to know all about it, even about my conversation with Kevin Warsh.

"The call [from Federal Reserve governor Kevin Warsh] was a signal that the 71-year-old Massey would be under strict federal supervision as he began perhaps the most challenging current board assignment in U.S. banking," his article said.

"The most challenging current board assignment in U.S. banking." That certainly got my attention.

"Under a relentless spotlight, Mr. Massey is trying to engineer a leadership makeover at the nation's largest bank by assets while responding to frustrated shareholders, aggressive regulators, and politicians agitated by the bank's $45 billion federal bailout," Dan's article announced. The article was co-authored with Joann Lublin, whom I never met.

I was shocked that Dan was aware of Kevin Warsh's call. How did he know that? Who would have told him about it?

The article went on to say, "Regulators had concerns about BofA board's lack of banking and financial expertise, its planning for a CEO successor and the depth of the bank's management team. Mr. Massey, Mr. Warsh made clear, would be well-suited to examine these issues."

I was stunned. Not just stunned, I was very upset. I would never have said all of that to Dan. Would people think I had told him these things?

This was just the beginning of Dan's surprises. I soon realized that he seemed to know everything. It was he, in fact, who revealed in the same article the manner in which I was chosen chairman, something that had always stumped me.

"Mr. Massey was elevated to the chairman's seat by a small group of directors who included current CEO Kenneth Lewis and Temple Sloan, a longtime supporter of Mr. Lewis," Dan and Lublin wrote. "The group met in the days leading up to an April 29th annual meeting, anticipating that shareholders might strip Mr. Lewis of his chairman's post."

To this day, Dan has never revealed his sources.

"I worked hard to cultivate them," he explained during our conversation years later.

Ken was the first person I called after the article was published.

"What do you think, Ken? How did it come across to the bank?"

"Well, Walter. You know, we're working on it. Our PR people are trying to control the message."

I was floored.

"What?? What do you mean, 'control the message,' Ken? Did I do some sort of damage that now has to be fixed?" I was quite distressed. I had raised my voice and didn't care.

Ken laughed. "Actually, it went very well, Walter. Everyone here really liked it."

"Well, that's a relief," I said.

It took several seconds for me to fully calm down. Ken was so dry, so matter-of-fact when he insinuated that I had created a mess that left the PR folks doing damage control, that I believed him. That was typical of his sense of humor.

I am not sure why, but I never asked Ken about Dan's account of how I was selected as chairman. Temple Sloan *did* chair the Executive Committee and had quite a bit of power on the board, so Dan's account was credible. But I still don't know if it was true.

CHAPTER TWENTY-FIVE
GETTING A HANDLE ON THINGS

The board now had eighteen members, but more exits and additions were still to come.

The dynamics of the board changed after we brought on the new members. The sense of accommodation — that easy willingness to reach an agreement — seemed diminished. For one thing, the existence of the Special Committee immediately became a matter of controversy, especially for the newest members of the board.

"How long will this Special Committee last?" some members asked.

"We need to end it. The sooner, the better," others said.

I said, I agreed. "We're working hard on our assignment, but it's really not up to us to dissolve the committee. Until the regulators agree that we are finished, we have no choice but to continue."

They understood this but still weren't satisfied.

"Why is a subgroup doing such very important work? The whole board should be working on these matters," members rebutted.

I replied that I heard them. They were good questions and valid arguments. "We will keep working to end the committee as expeditiously as possible," was all I could offer.

We were walking a fine line. Boards have to act as full boards. It's not healthy to have a subgroup making such important decisions unless the full board expressly authorizes it. The full board had indeed given authorization for the Special Committee. But as some directors noted, the newly constituted board did not give that authorization. Its predecessor did.

My colleagues and I continued to defend the committee's existence.

"Believe me; no one wants the Special Committee to exist in perpetuity. The Feds certainly don't. But we have an obligation to complete the work we agreed to," I insisted.

Another committee member spoke up. "Walter is right. We have an agreement with the Feds. The Special Committee simply cannot go out of existence until it completes the prescribed work."

I wanted everyone to feel they were involved in the work anyway.

I said, "As you know, we are keeping all board members informed of our work. No one wants this to be over more than me, I assure you. I think the work is going well, but you should ask the regulators directly when they meet with us."

They weren't all disgruntled, although one or two of them seemed more petulant than the others. All of them wanted to be assured that the committee was going to have an end date. So did we.

I felt it was important to exhibit a tone of accommodation. We needed to create a new board that was a collegial, cohesive entity, but as long as this subgroup of old board members existed, endowed with the power and authority it had, it would be difficult to achieve the harmonious atmosphere we needed to build that cohesiveness. This was a challenge we had to work through.

The Special Committee continued to meet separately, but we always reported back to the full board. And Jennifer, Lisa, and Grace met regularly with the board to give their independent assessment of how things were going.

But unease persisted. The composition of the board's standing committees was another point of contention. Board members were justifiably concerned, not only about who would serve on the committees, but more importantly, who would chair the committees.

Committee memberships, and particularly committee chairs, are very important assignments because the majority of the board's work is done in committees. This is true of any corporate board and most nonprofits. Compensation and Benefit, as the name indicates, recommends the salaries of senior officers, including the CEO's salary. Corporate Governance recruits and recommends new board members and determines the committee structure and composition of committees. While these two usually are considered the board's most powerful committees, the Audit and Risk committees are most important to the regulators.

Every committee, therefore, including the membership and chair — Is significant. Precisely for this reason, committee memberships should be determined by much more than the desire or willingness of a board member to serve. Expertise and experience in the committee's scope of work are critical determining factors. That's why Audit committee members, for example, are required to be 'financial experts' or 'financially literate,' as defined by the SEC, the Securities and Exchange Commission.

I was acutely aware that the Fed wanted us to reconstitute the board because it felt we did not have enough members with banking and financial expertise. So, I knew we had to tread carefully on committee memberships, making sure to put the right people in the right places. In the past, when Ken was chairman, the Executive Committee made many of these decisions, as it was empowered to do. However, the Special Committee and the new board decided early on to abolish the Executive Committee so that all important decisions would be made by the full board. But in the absence of the Executive Committee, the question arose as to how new committee assignments would be made before a new Governance Committee was established.

To address this, I relied on the statement in the Stress Test press release that the Special Committee "is charged with reviewing and recommending changes in all aspects of the board's activities, from the structure and charters of its standing committees, to board meetings and agendas, to board composition and size." So, the Special Committee discussed and came to an agreement on committee assignments. I then called directors to inform them of our intentions and to request that they serve on, and in some cases, chair particular committees.

Most of the directors I called readily agreed to the Committee's requests. Others had their own preferences and responded with a statement like, "That's okay if you need me there, Walter, but I'm more interested in Audit than Credit. If possible, that's the committee I'd rather be on." We almost always found a mutually satisfactory outcome when that happened.

Only one obstreperous new director questioned the entire process. He accused me of trying to stack committees with continuing directors and members of the Special Committee. On one phone call, he challenged me on this issue in a language and tone that I felt questioned not only my choices, but also impugned my integrity.

He opened with, "Walter, I think you are trying to manipulate the committee assignments to put in your buddies from the special committee."

I bristled, resenting his condemnatory tone.

"That's not true. I have no reason to do that," I replied tersely.

"Well, I don't believe that!"

That shredded any effort I might have made to be civil.

"Are you accusing me of lying about this?" My voice was as harsh as his.

"I am telling you that I don't think you are doing all this above board, and you have some ulterior motive!" he rejoined, his voice rising.

"That's not true! And I resent your speaking to me like that!"

My head was beginning to throb. Never in my professional career had my integrity been so blatantly questioned.

"Don't you ever speak to me like that again!" I shouted into the phone. I was standing on the deck of our home on Cape Cod, angrier than I had been in years. I'm sure my voice carried all the way to the beach.

"I think we should end this conversation," I said through gritted teeth.

"Fine with me!"

I clicked off, painfully missing the satisfaction of slamming an old-fashioned phone into its cradle. It took me at least an hour to calm down. I did what I had learned to do when I felt my blood pressure was in danger of rising: I exercised. I went for a long, exhausting bike ride on the winding back roads in our area. It helped enormously. I calmed down eventually, determined to move on.

I'm sure I was not completely blameless in whatever led that board member to misinterpret my actions. Placing people on the committees they preferred, while making sure we had the expertise we needed in the right places, was a complicated process, and could be subject to misinterpretation. This particular director was one of the most experienced and admired bankers among the new members. We had worked hard to get him to join us, and I valued his contributions. After our irate exchange, however, he and I never established a close personal relationship. But, we kept it professional and continued to work together.

In the end, we populated all the committees and assigned chairmanships. We were now able to conduct the business of the bank.

I had an office in Charlotte and another in Chicago. Alice Herald worked with me almost full-time. She was a lawyer by training. Before I asked for her support, I explained to her that in working for the Special Committee and for me, she would become privy to information and discussions that had to be kept confidential, even from her supervisors at the bank.

"I know this will put you in an awkward, and even potentially vulnerable position, Alice. Please think carefully about it before you decide to come on board," I said to her.

She did not hesitate.

"I hear you, Walter, and I'd still like the assignment."

Ed Herlihy was another gem of a human being during that grueling period. He didn't look like the brilliant and successful New York lawyer he was; his better-known partner, Marty Lipton, looked the part.

Ed was a large, somewhat rumpled-looking guy with a polite, friendly, even avuncular manner. He wore round glasses and had thick, salt-and-pepper hair, a patch of which always seemed to fall waywardly in a soft wave on his forehead. He was one of the best listeners I'd ever worked with. He asked deep questions — and there were many — that forced me to thoroughly think through situations. An excellent example of this was when he asked me, "Have you thought through how you are going to do a succession plan without creating an impression that you are moving toward getting rid of Ken?"

Ed didn't bombard you with his own opinions. Yet, his insights and knowledge of people and institutions were profound and widely recognized. I had all of his phone numbers — office, home, mobile — and I called him often. Sometimes just to shoot the breeze, other times to get his feedback on an idea I'd had. He always made himself available to me — evenings, weekends, holidays, even when he was in a meeting or on vacation.

One of my first calls to him is as fresh in my mind as if it happened just yesterday. It was the call I made when I was struggling to come up with the precise language I wanted to use in the Stress Test press release. I wanted his take on the idea I'd had.

I called him as soon as I got out of bed, about seven in the morning Chicago time, or about eight in New York on May 4th. His secretary answered.

"Good morning. Ed Herlihy's office. Christine here, may I help you?"

I hardly knew Christine then, but I eventually got to know her very well as I continued to work closely with Ed.

"Hi. This is Walter Massey. I'm calling to speak to Ed. Is he available?"

"He's in a meeting, but I'm sure he will want to speak with you, Dr. Massey. Just a minute, I'll find him."

Sure enough, Ed was on the line a few minutes later. He greeted me in a warm, cheerful voice.

"Walter! You okay? What's up?"

As usual, he listened attentively and made thoughtful observations, which were very helpful.

Apart from my fellow Special Committee members, many others helped me personally during my tenure as chairman, but Ed and Alice topped the list.

As October approached, I felt we were getting a handle on things. Our committee was working well together. The newly instituted board committees were functioning well. We had recruited excellent new board members, including Robert Scully, an experienced, well-respected banker who had served as co-president at Morgan Stanley and as a managing director at Lehman Brothers and Salomon Brothers. When he joined our board, he was also chairman of the New York City region of Teach for America (TFA). We hit it off from the beginning, and my experience with TFA when I was president at Morehouse, led me to get to know him fairly well.

The Fed and the OCC seemed to think we were making good progress. I continued to speak with Lisa, Jennifer, and Grace almost every week, and regularly with Jeff Lacker.

As the weeks went by, I began to feel that the toughest parts of our assignment had passed. At the very least, the structures had been put in place for the work that needed to be done. The challenges we now faced included integrating Merrill's huge staff, changing key management positions, and keeping up the bank's morale. We were still operating under the onerous restrictions of the TARP loans, and the Treasury Department's 'pay czar,' Kenneth Feinberg, tightly controlled our compensation levels. We also faced many lawsuits against both the bank and its directors.

At one point, Jeff Lacker asked to meet with the Special Committee for an update on our work. I had kept him informed through phone calls, but this was the first time we would meet in person since our meeting in Richmond. Thankfully, we did not have to go to Richmond. Jeff came to us in Charlotte instead.

It definitely was a friendlier, more relaxed meeting than that infamous one in Richmond. By now, we were pretty comfortable with one another. This time around, we were more collaborators than adversaries. The meeting did not last very long. Jeff told us that he was very pleased with the progress we had made and that he was impressed with how hard we were working. As he was leaving, he paused at the door, looked back at us, and in a very serious voice, said, "I want to thank you for all you are doing for the country."

With that, he left, closing the door firmly behind him.

I think we were all stunned. We looked at each other as if to say, "Did you hear what I just heard?"

I had never thought of our work in that way. It dawned on me then that Jeff was feeling as much pressure as we were. If we failed to secure the future of Bank of America, Jeff, too, would have failed. Indeed, the Fed itself would be seen as failing.

From that time onward, I felt very differently about our work. I believe all of us on the Committee did. We were not simply carrying out a mandate from regulators. We were playing a major role in holding together the financial infrastructure of the country.

By early September, I had begun to imagine that the next months of my chairmanship, which would last until I retired in May 2010, might feel more like a normal chairman's job. We had brought in several new directors, were well on our way to raising the thirty-four billion the Stress Test said we needed, and changed our senior risk management structure and risk reporting procedures. I felt we were at least moving out of our crisis period. The stock had stopped its steep decline and had settled around ten to twelve dollars per share.

Not so slowly, but surely, we checked off the list of items the Fed had presented to us two days after I took over as chairman. Maybe we would have time to at least catch our breath.

But we were constantly in the press. And we had an inordinate number of leaks. I never learned the source of the leaks then. I do know I dreaded each morning opening *The Wall St. Journal*, fearing yet another leak. Invariably, its articles contained information on the bank's relationship with the feds, the work of the committee, or scrutiny of Ken. I've often said that Dan Fitzpatrick must have been a fly on the wall at every board meeting.

Yet, things seemed to be falling into place. Trouble was, they never really did.

We had done much of what we had been asked to do. Directors were completing their assignments — Tom and Chad on succession planning, and Frank and Charles on risk assessment. The board was finally coming together, and the new members were making wonderful contributions.

We were moving along, and I was feeling pretty good.

Then Steele Alphin called, and we were in crisis mode all over again.

CHAPTER TWENTY-SIX
KEN LEWIS WANTS
TO RESIGN

The phone call from Steele Alphin that summer was almost as unsettling as Chad Gifford's call from Croatia the day after I was elected chairman.

Shirley and I were on Cape Cod for most of the summer, and I had been commuting to New York and Charlotte for meetings. Our two grandchildren were staying with us. Eva, our granddaughter, was eight. Her brother, Artem, was six. They lived in Moscow with their mother, who is Russian. She and our youngest son, Eric, had divorced. They had met as students at the University of Chicago.

The grandchildren had been spending their summers with us since Artem was three, and Eva was five. Cape Cod is a kids' heaven in the summer. There are dunes to bump around; all kinds of trails to hike; tidal pools to splash about in; seashells and clams to hunt; and a wildlife sanctuary, aquarium, and theme museums to explore, such as the Whydah Pirate Museum which houses an authentic shipwreck. Along the seashore, hundreds of species of birds create their annual kaleidoscope of flitter and flutter. Out in the water, whales frolic, seals sunbathe, seagulls swoop, and dolphins leap — plenty of novelty for the grandkids, and for Shirley and me, alike.

Back on land, there are magic shows, a children's theater, an inflatable amusement park, endless days of face painting, storytelling, scavenger hunts, kite flying, bowling, and arcade games. There are also ice cream parlors galore.

So, Shirley and I were not simply relaxing on the beach alone or hitting balls on the tennis court all summer.

"The grandchildren certainly keep us in shape," I said to Shirley one evening.

We'd had this conversation before. As usual, we were relaxing on the front deck, enjoying the starry night with a glass of wine. Crickets sang.

Eva and Artem had gone to bed, finally. A full day of high-spirited fun and games had worn them out. It had worn us out, too.

Shirley chuckled. "They really do. Mentally and physically. Those kids are curious about everything."

"Thank God we're still healthy and active enough to keep up with them."

"You can say that again."

"Yeah. They sure help me to take my mind off the bank."

"And not to mention keeping your blood pressure down."

"We should have skipped having children and gone straight to the grandkids."

Shirley and I often joke in this way, as I'm sure most grandparents do.

Steele Alphin, as I've noted, was Ken Lewis's closest confidant at the bank. I'd come to know him quite well. As the chief administrative officer, he oversaw human resources, compensation, and other important functions. Many people believed he was the bank's most powerful person after Ken.

Steele was also Ken's close friend, loyal to him as a blade to a hilt. But from working with him in these stressful situations, I'd learned that his first loyalty was to the bank, the institution he had helped Ken to build.

He called on Saturday, the 26th of September, early in the evening. I will never forget that date. The evening was cool, the temperature in the fifties. The grandkids had gone back to Moscow, and Shirley and I were packing up for the drive home to Chicago.

"Hey, Walter," Steele began. "How was your summer?"

I wasn't surprised to hear from Steele. He called fairly regularly to keep in touch or to ask about specific issues. It was not unusual for him to call on a weekend. We all worked seven days a week.

After a few pleasantries, he broached the real reason for his call in a more serious tone.

"Ken asked me to arrange a meeting in Boston with him on Monday. That would be Monday, the 28th. Just you, Chad, Tom, and him."

"This sounds urgent, Steele. Is there anything I should know before we meet?"

"Well, you should know that Ken has been talking about retiring early. I am sure that's what he wants to talk about."

"*What!* Did he say why?"

I was alarmed and didn't try to camouflage it. A sudden departure by Ken was the last thing we needed.

"He just seems to think it is time." Steele sounded glum.

"Well, we will talk about it. I just hope it isn't so."

Throughout the troubles of the past few months, beginning with the meeting at the Fed in Richmond, Ken had retained the board's support. At no time did I feel pressure from our regulators, or from the Treasury, for him to resign.

Chad, Tom, and I met Ken that Monday in Boston at a private club where Chad was a member. I'd had a brief conversation on the phone with Chad and Tom before we met Ken, and we had agreed that we would hear him out and not make any premature judgments. But it is fair to say that we were gravely concerned.

The four of us dined in a private room. Ken was neither tense nor upset. Quite the contrary, he was very relaxed — a man at peace with himself. We chatted about how he had spent the summer in Aspen and kidded him about the beard he had grown. The beard was a big surprise. He didn't look 'bankerly' at all. In hindsight, we should have taken that as a giant hint of what was to come.

Eventually, we got around to the reason for the meeting. Ken said he had thought very carefully about his future, and he wanted to retire at the end of the calendar year.

Steele had warned us that this was coming, but we still felt very uneasy and troubled. I had thought Ken might ask our advice on his plans, or that he would stay at least until the next annual meeting in May 2010. If he were staying until then, we could have planned to elect my successor as chairman and his successor as chief executive at the same time.

"Why do you want to do that, Ken?" I said. "You have the full support of the board. Don't you want to give it some more thought to make sure this really is something you want to do?"

Chad and Tom spoke up with similar comments, noting the work he had done over the years to make the bank better. But Ken was resolute.

"My mind is made up. I'm doing what I believe is best for the bank and for me."

"We don't think so," I said. Chad and Tom nodded in agreement.

Choosing the CEO is the single most important thing a board does. It's no trivial undertaking. However, we may have felt about Ken's performance — and we felt good about it — the thought of having to conduct a search for a new CEO was daunting, to say the least. For here we were, with a newly constituted board, still deeply immersed in our Fed-mandated work. This was a predicament that we had to deal with not only delicately, but also quickly because Ken's decision was likely to be leaked once others learned of it.

We had suffered vexing leaks all summer. Dan Fitzpatrick, the *Wall Street Journal* reporter, was relentless. He constantly focused on our board's deliberations and wrote at length about them with unusual accuracy. It became so difficult to carry out our work in confidence that at one point earlier in the summer, Steele was driven to call me.

"Walter, I hate to say this, but everyone is worried about the leaks, and some of the senior team are concerned that you may be the one talking. I know it's not true, but that reporter seems to know everything," he said.

I heard the discomfort in his voice and inwardly commiserated with him. But it really upset, angered me even, that there were individuals who felt I could, and *would*, betray the confidence of the board's deliberations.

"That's a hell of a concern for some of the senior team to have, Steele!" I may have raised my voice. "Why would I want to do something like that?"

"I absolutely believe you, Walter. But I had to let you know what some people are saying." Steele sounded genuinely contrite.

"Yeah? Steele, you know me, so I hope you let those people know that this is something I would never do."

"I did and will keep telling them I don't believe it. But it is a problem."

I calmed down. "Thanks, Steele, and thanks for telling me this."

We never found the source of the leaks. They remained a stubborn, irksome undercurrent throughout all of our work.

Leaks or no leaks, however, Ken's decision forced us to act. We had to schedule a meeting of the full board as soon as possible to discuss how we would proceed and to prepare an alert to our major constituents. We had to notify the government — the Federal Reserve, the OCC, FDIC, and Treasury — all in the appropriate order. It was important to respect the sensitivities of these various parties. We did not need another reason to be publicly castigated. Moreover, the resignation or retirement of a CEO is a legally 'reportable event,' requiring public notice through the 'timely' filing of an 8-K form with the SEC. We also had to prepare press releases and communications to employees. Ken would inform his senior team at the appropriate time.

We wanted to avoid another leak at all costs.

I asked Alice to schedule a call-in board meeting for that Thursday, October 1st, three days after Chad, Tom, and I met with Ken. The three days would give staff time to prepare the necessary announcements and filings that would have to be made immediately after the board met.

Sure enough, as leaks would have it, I got a call from Anne Finucane on the morning of September 30th, the day before the scheduled board meeting. Anne was head of corporate communications at the bank. She went straight to the point.

"The New York Times has the story about Ken's retirement, Walter. It'll be in tomorrow's early edition," Anne said.

She was as calm and composed as always. I, on the other hand, was mortified.

"What! How could this happen? Who did this? Will it never stop?"

"Here is what we have to do to stay ahead of this story. We need to move the board meeting to this afternoon," Anne said evenly.

Anne was a remarkable woman. She could be funny and lighthearted, but she was always focused on the task at hand. I found her background very interesting. Raised in Massachusetts in a large Irish family, she started out working in the arts for then-Boston Mayor Kevin White. She made the move into banking in 1995 when she went to Fleet to work in corporate affairs and marketing. Although she had no financial or banking training at the time, she soon proved how smart and valuable she was in understanding and dealing with the public, including members of Congress.

At one point, during the Special Committee's deliberations, we seriously considered hiring a public relations specialist to work directly with our committee. However, we decided fairly quickly, at Chad's and Ken's urging, that Anne was fully capable of handling the delicate job of representing the committee and the board, as well as the bank management. This proved to be a wise decision. Anne was unflappable.

We couldn't afford to have the other board members read about Ken's early departure in the press before they heard from Ken himself, so we hurriedly moved up our board meeting to 5 p.m. that very afternoon. Amazingly, everyone was available and joined in on the call. Ken was visiting with staff in New York City at the time and made the call from the new Bank of America Tower, a twelve-hundred-foot, environment-friendly skyscraper located at One Bryant Park in the city's Midtown.

Shortly before the board meeting got underway, Ken had delivered the news to the executives who reported to him, including CFO Joe Price; Brian Moynihan, president of Consumer and Small Business banking; Sally Krawcheck, president of Global Wealth and Investment Management; Tom Montag, president of Global Banking and Markets; and Greg Curl, chief risk officer.

I opened the session and thanked everyone for making themselves available on such short notice. I assured them that the matter we had to discuss arose unexpectedly and was of a most critical nature, hence the short notice.

I didn't know what the board expected to hear, but I was certain it was not what Ken was about to tell them.

I turned the meeting over to Ken. As he had done to Chad, Tom, and me in Boston, he explained that he wanted to retire at the end of the year. He stressed that it was a personal decision.

"Nothing external precipitated my decision. I always felt I would know when it was the appropriate time to leave, and I feel this is an appropriate time," he said.

He sounded amiable, but I knew he would entertain no argument. His mind was made up.

We were on a conference call, so it was difficult to read the individual reactions to his announcement. Nevertheless, the interjections and the tone of the discussion that followed, indicated that board members generally were startled, and at the same time, understanding of Ken's position.

In the official press release, Ken conveyed that he was leaving the bank on sound footing. True to character, he gave no hint of regret in his statement and made no apology for decisions he had made as chairman and CEO. Instead, he projected only complete confidence in the bank's ability to withstand the tests of the times.

"Bank of America is well-positioned to meet the continuing challenges of the economy and markets," he stated. "I am particularly heartened by the results that are emerging from the decisions and initiatives of the difficult past year-and-a-half. The Merrill Lynch and Countrywide integrations are on track and returning value already. Our board of directors and our senior management include more talent, and more diversity of talent, than at any time in this company's history. We are in a position to begin to repay the federal government's TARP investments. For these reasons, I decided now is the time to begin to transition to the next generation of leadership at the Bank of America."

In my own statement for the release, I sought to affirm both Ken's positive legacy and the picture he painted of the condition in which he was leaving the bank.

"Ken Lewis was a key architect in building a truly global financial franchise," I said. "We are on a solid path to the future. The board will be moving in a deliberate and expeditious manner to select a worthy successor to Ken Lewis."

Ken wrote a farewell letter to the bank's employees in which he reiterated that he had not been forced to retire. "To my teammates," the letter began, "Some will suggest that I am leaving under pressure or because of questions regarding the Merrill deal. I will simply say that this was my decision and mine alone."

I can't say how the 'teammates' reacted, but as we interviewed senior executives later, it became clear that people were simply trying to move ahead. I'm sure Ken's letter was unsettling, but the employees had a bank to run. There was so much to do that I don't think anyone had time to wallow in gloom. Not even Ken's farewell could detract them from their work.

As expected, Ken's letter was leaked to *The Wall Street Journal*. Its contents first appeared in a Dan Fitzpatrick article, which other news organizations referenced in their own reports.

The press had a field day with the news. They hounded board members, including me, for interviews. Bob Stickler, the bank's spokesman, generally ran interference with reporters, emphasizing that Ken made the decision on his own and not as a result of pressure from law enforcement authorities, regulators, or the newly overhauled board. This was true. Never, in the regulators' insistence that the bank must improve its risk management and succession planning, was there any pressure for Ken to resign.

Dan Fitzpatrick's lengthy article was replete with information gleaned directly from the board's closed-door discussions. Allegedly, he got the information from 'a person close' to Ken. His article was headlined "Bank of America Chief Resigns Under Fire," with the long subtitle, "Lewis to Leave at Year End as Lender Faces New York Probe of Merrill Deal; Fed Up After a Year of Criticism; Successor Unclear."

"The board had told Mr. Lewis it wanted to know how long he planned to stay," Dan wrote. "He indicated that he would stay through 2010, this person said, but he changed his mind during a vacation to Aspen, Colo., in late August."

The article continued, "Mr. Lewis had been in discussions with the board about the appropriate time to step down after directors had made it clear they wanted a time frame, said the person close to him. Initially, he wanted to stay until the company repaid its forty-five billion dollars in federal bailout funds, and returned to earning thirty billion dollars a year. That plan changed following his return from vacation, which didn't leave him feeling as energized as it usually did, he told the person close to him. He had come to the conclusion that he was 'really tired of all the mud that was being piled on him,' said this person ... Even as the board backed Mr. Lewis publicly, there were signs that his interests and the bank's were diverging."

I was flabbergasted. Where on earth did he get that last bit? What signs was he talking about? I certainly saw no such signs, nor was I made aware of any.

In a conversation with Dan, years later, I asked him about his sources. He still would not reveal them, but he did say his greatest disappointment was that he did not get the scoop on Ken's retirement. *The New York Times* did, as Anne Finucane had warned.

Given the troubles Bank of America faced, and the pummeling it was taking in the press, it was easy to forget that Ken's prior accomplishments had earned him the industry's highest accolades, just as it was easy to overlook the fact that he had remained loyal and committed to this single organization for four decades. Although many people thought he was right to retire — and sooner rather than later — personally, I felt a genuine mix of sadness and admiration for Ken.

"He's had a big target on his chest for the whole Merrill Lynch deal, and I can only imagine the emotional stress he's endured," a research analyst named Alan Villalon said in an interview with the Associated Press.

Villalon worked at Minneapolis-based First American Funds, which owned Bank of America stock.

About a month later, *Institutional Investor* magazine had this to say: "The bitter irony for Lewis is that just as his own position was becoming untenable, Merrill's performance was beginning to justify the deal. The New York-based investment bank is set to generate about one-quarter of the combined firm's net income and nearly 20 percent of revenues this year, based on company filings ... The investment bank generated $1.84 billion in net income in the first six months of the year, or about 25 percent of BofA's $7.47 billion in earnings for the period, according to company filings. The investment banking unit had revenues of $12.1 billion over the period, representing about 18 percent of the group's overall revenues of $68.5 billion."

These numbers were indisputable. *Institutional Investor*'s assessment was dead-on.

Predictably, Ken's detractors cheered the news of what they insisted on calling his 'resignation.' Some of the bank's investors were still on the warpath and made it clear that they could not wait for him to leave. They hadn't forgiven Ken for the Merrill purchase, which shrank the value of their holdings when the bank's stock price fell. Several news organizations carried a statement from Change to Win (CtW) Investment Group. CtW owned less than one percent of the bank's shares, but they were one of the most truculent lobbyists for Ken's removal, both as chairman and CEO.

"Ken Lewis's resignation as CEO is the overdue but inevitable result of the overwhelming shareholder opposition registered at Bank of America's 2009 annual meeting," the group announced through its spokesperson. "The onus is now on the board of directors to engage with shareholders to name a successor who can quickly restore the bank's credibility with investors, regulators, and Congress."

This was absolutely correct. As chairman, I felt that onus deeply.

CHAPTER TWENTY-SEVEN
NO TIME TO LOSE

With Ken's year-end departure a grim reality, the board's most urgent tasks were to establish a process to choose his successor and reassure investors that the bank was stable. Chad and Tom were deep into our succession planning effort, having already interviewed the senior management, and assessed the strengths and weaknesses of the bank's leadership, but their work was not yet finished. We, therefore, had no clear succession plan in place.

We lost no time to accomplish what we needed to do. After Ken dropped his bombshell at the board meeting, I asked him to leave the meeting so that the board members could discuss how we were going to proceed.

"Well, we need to make sure we have a thorough search and look outside as well as inside the bank," one member said after Ken left.

"Definitely. But maybe we should also be working on both a short- and long-term plan. Suppose we can't complete the search before Ken leaves," another said.

This was a valid point. The Fed and the OCC had been pushing the Special Committee to complete the succession plan, including an emergency plan. We hadn't done that, so we now had to develop a plan *and* conduct a full-blown search at the same time.

197

Since the meeting with Ken in Boston, I had been giving a lot of thought to how best to organize the search for his successor. Clearly, we needed a search committee. But who should be on it? And who should chair it? I felt such a committee would function most efficiently if I chaired it because I had established good relations with the regulators and senior management. But I was not sure that the entire board would agree to this.

"We have to set up a search committee right away, and I think it is appropriate that I chair it," I told the board. "I'll ask some of you to serve on that committee. We want to do this as quickly as we can, but also very thoroughly."

Thankfully, no one disagreed.

I wanted to make sure our new members were represented on the Search Committee, so I chose Charles "Chad" Holliday, the recently retired CEO of DuPont, and Don Powell, former head of the FDIC. I had gotten to know Chad Holliday before he joined the board. When I was on the BP board of directors, we tried to recruit him to the board, and I was assigned to interview him and make the request. He could not join BP at that time because of other commitments. So I was very pleased that he consented to join the Bank of America board when we recruited him.

I did not know Don at all before he came on board, but he was already proving to be an excellent director.

Tom May and Chad Gifford were logical choices since they were already involved in planning the succession. I added Tom Ryan, the chief executive of CVS, who chaired the board's Compensation Committee. Compensation naturally would be a key concern of potential candidates. We were still operating under TARP restrictions, so we were limited in what we could pay a new CEO.

I was now chairing two committees that met with great frequency, the Special Committee and the Search Committee. Tom May and Chad Gifford were also on both committees.

We still had the ongoing business of the bank to conduct. I kept up my regular meetings with Ken, during which he was always pretty relaxed. He was still CEO, and I was still chairman of the bank. The bank had to keep working, and the full Board still met regularly — very often, in fact.

We decided at the very beginning to conduct a broad search, interviewing both internal and external candidates. Neither the Fed nor the White House had ever put pressure on us to select an outsider, an insider, or a particular individual, as the public speculated. But Kevin Warsh did call me on Friday, the day after the announcement about Ken.

I remember the call vividly. I was sitting in my car in the parking lot outside a health club in Hyde Park where we lived, having just attended a Pilates class. As I noted earlier, regular, focused exercise had been an important part of my stress-control regimen for years. Shirley had persuaded me to try Pilates. She introduced me to her instructor, Marylee Bussard, whose studio was right in our neighborhood, and I had quickly become a devotee. Beyond reducing stress, I found that Pilates made me more flexible and improved my range of motion, which helped my tennis game tremendously.

"Walter, I just spoke with Ben about the announcement," Kevin said, as I made myself more comfortable behind the wheel. I knew he was referring to Federal Reserve Chairman Ben Bernanke.

"We've been discussing Ken's unexpected decision to leave and your board's plans to name a successor."

Kevin spoke in that now-familiar casual but deadly serious tone.

"Ben doesn't think the timing of these developments presents the most elegant solution to the bank's problems. It would have been better if you'd been able to have one big announcement naming Ken's successor at the same time you announced his retirement," Kevin continued. "But, it's okay."

It doesn't present the most elegant solution. I've carried around that statement in my mind for years. It resonated with me because, in theoretical physics, a solution to a problem should not only be 'correct,' but it also should be 'elegant.'

"I agree the timing is bad. However, the circumstances forced us to act as we did," I said.

I closed my eyes and sighed — inaudibly. What a relief! Bernanke could have been a lot more upset than Kevin made him seem. After all, the situation with Ken and Bank of America only added to his worries about the whole banking system. Volatility may be good for traders but not so for regulators. They prefer stability.

"I'm sure I don't have to tell you that it's the board's job to pick a new CEO, not the Federal Reserve's or any other outside groups'. But as the bank's primary regulator and supervisory agency, we want to be assured that the board will conduct a thorough, professional, credible search," Kevin said.

I responded quickly and firmly. "I can assure you that's our intention, Kevin. We see no other way to proceed."

"You can't waste any time on this, Walter. A lot of people will be watching to see who you will choose to succeed Ken. Bank of America needs the strongest possible leadership right now."

"Of course."

"We all have a great deal of confidence in you and the board, Walter. I'm sure you'll work this through."

I felt even more relieved and heartened. "Thanks, Kevin. We won't let you down."

I was really pleased to hear Kevin emphasize that picking the new CEO was the board's responsibility and not the Fed's. The press was already speculating that the government would control the search process.

Then, out of the blue, I received a phone call from the director with whom I'd had the run-in about committee assignments. I assumed he was going to chastise me about the Search Committee or some aspect of the search process. Instead, he was cordial and made some very helpful suggestions.

"We're very lucky to have Chad [Gifford] on the board. He could do the job for a few months if we find ourselves in a pinch," he said.

I was genuinely surprised. Chad was one of the "buddies" he had accused me of favoring in the committee membership appointment process. As I noted earlier, he was one of our most experienced directors and continued to demonstrate that at the most unusual times.

Just as I was getting into a routine of chairing these two hardworking committees, another ugly issue came to the forefront: the ongoing, persistent, and very public investigation by the attorney general of New York, Andrew Cuomo. Cuomo wanted to know if our board knew of additional losses at Merrill after the merger was signed, and whether we knew about the billions of dollars in bonus payments to Merrill executives before the deal closed. His office suggested that members of the Audit Committee and other directors probably knew about the losses and bonus payments before shareholders voted to approve the deal in December. It also planned to ask board members about the pressure the government might have brought to bear on the bank's decision on when to disclose the bonuses and losses to shareholders, and whether government officials said they would remove management and the board if the bank didn't proceed with the deal.

"Did the boards of directors of our largest financial institutions protect the rights of shareholders? Were they misled, or were they little more than rubber stamps for management's decision-making? We intend to find out what Bank of America's board knew and when they knew it during the Merrill Lynch merger," Cuomo said in a statement that was widely reported by the press.

He threatened to subpoena and depose many directors who were on the board during the Merrill acquisition, including those who had subsequently left the board. I was one of those deposed, along with Tom May, who chaired the Audit Committee; retired Army General Tommy Franks; real estate executive William Barnet; and venture capital executive John Collins. Tom and I were the only directors still on the board who were deposed. Cuomo's office also announced that both

IN THE EYE OF THE STORM

Ken and Joe Price, the bank's chief financial officer, might be criminally indicted.

Being accused of *criminal* activity was a brand new territory and presented a new level of crisis. Up to that point, no one had been accused of criminal actions. The bank at all times cooperated with the attorney general's office, but we took the position that there was no basis for charges against either the company or individual members of the management team and certainly not criminal charges.

Having to respond to Cuomo at this time was a most unwelcome diversion. We were in October. Ken would be leaving at the end of December. We had no time to lose in finding his successor.

Being deposed was a harrowing, exhausting experience for me. It took a full day to practice for my deposition after days of preparation, and the deposition itself took another full day. Giving a deposition is a very serious undertaking, especially when it's to a government agency. You are under oath and subject to charges of perjury if you do not answer all questions truthfully. Even inadvertent mistakes sometimes lead to perjury charges. It is not uncommon for individuals to be charged with perjury, even if they are never convicted of the original charges for which they are deposed.

Justifiably, the lawyers assigned to represent the bank's directors in Cuomo's investigation insisted on extensive preparation and practice before we gave our depositions. For the entire day of Thursday, October 13th, I was subjected to a mock deposition at the offices of Davis Polk & Wardell. The lawyers asked me every possible question they thought the Attorney General's Office could put to me.

"Suppose I can't remember something I am asked about?" I queried anxiously.

"Just say, 'I don't recall,' or, 'I don't remember that.' You cannot be made to remember something that you don't recall," one of the attorneys advised. "The problem that academics have — I am sorry to say, Walter — is that they want to show

how smart they are. They do not like to admit they don't remember some things. This is not an IQ test. This is an official investigation. It is perfectly fine to say, 'I'm sorry, I just don't remember.'"

I felt chastened. "This is going to take how long?"

"Can't say. It's up to them. One day. Maybe two. We've told them that you were only available for these two days and that your appearance is voluntary. You were not subpoenaed, which means you were requested, not ordered, to appear. So, I am sure it won't be longer than that."

"Well, I have to go to the bathroom quite frequently. What do I do when I have to go?"

"We will be in the room with you. Just let one of us know."

The actual deposition took place in a small, cramped, sparsely furnished room at the United States District Court Southern District of New York. It was a room with no windows. It smelled of stale air. *They must have deliberately chosen this room to make me uncomfortable. They probably do the same thing to all of their victims,* I thought resentfully.

I sat at a table stacked with documents. Three stone-faced officials from the AG's office sat directly across from me. My two attorneys sat behind me. A court reporter at one end of the table recorded the proceedings.

It was not a friendly environment.

I was sworn in and agreed to testify truthfully. Frequently during the session, one of the AG officials would hand me a document extracted from the stacks on the table and would state something to the effect of, "Let the record show that the document we have before us is SG224. Is that the number of the document you have, Dr. Massey?"

"Yes, it is."

Questions about the document followed.

"Do you recognize this document?"

"Yes, I do."

"Please tell us what it is."

"It is the minutes of the January 2009 board meeting."

"Please look at page two, line fourteen, where it states that the board discussed the fourth-quarter results of Merrill Lynch. Do you remember that discussion?"

And so it went, on and on with irritating tedium through several stacks of documents for almost seven hours. Cuomo's team was ready to pounce on the slightest discrepancy in my testimony, and any discrepancies between my testimony and that of the other directors. They had a theory to prove: that "the Board of Directors of Bank of America did not protect the rights of the shareholders," and were "little more than rubber stamps for management decision making."

I was their prey.

It was a physically and mentally draining experience. I was nervous throughout, so much so that I was surprised when, during breaks, my attorneys would say, "You're doing great, Walter. Everything is going very well."

"Really? Well, it doesn't seem like it to me," I would retort.

I couldn't wait to get away from the whole scene.

I had met Andrew Cuomo when he was the Secretary of the U.S. Department of Housing and Urban Development between 1997 and 2001. He had come to Morehouse to celebrate the beginning of a program that the Atlanta Housing Authority had put in place to renovate public housing. One of the target areas was right across the street from Morehouse, Spelman College, and the Morehouse School of Medicine. The three schools had worked with the Atlanta Housing Authority to transform the area with new housing and other amenities. I was president of Morehouse at the time, and we had a celebratory meeting there with Cuomo. He was young then — very vibrant, very outgoing, very charismatic. He was so impressive that after meeting him, I thought he should run for president of the country and said so to him.

So, I had these warm feelings towards Cuomo, but I must say they withered away during the Bank of America depositions.

The entire proceeding really went well for the bank; it seemed. The AG's office did not pursue these issues after all the depositions were taken. This was a huge relief for all of us.

CHAPTER TWENTY-EIGHT
THE SEARCH

The search took much longer than I anticipated. I kept Kevin, Jennifer, Lisa, Grace, and Jeff informed of our progress throughout. We also made sure, mainly through Don Powell, that Sheila Bair, the chairman of the FDIC, was kept in the loop. Don was on good terms with her, having been a former head of the FDIC himself.

It was a joy to work with Don and to get to know him. Handsome, with silvery grey hair, eyes set deep under generous brows, and a soft western accent that was 'not too citified and not too country,' he seemed perfect for a Hollywood casting of a Texas businessman. His firm handshake complemented the way he'd look you directly in the eye. Don was a fount of humorous Texas wisdom. An experienced former banker and regulator, he added substantially to all of our work.

The FDIC was not one of our key regulatory agencies, but it had the final say on whether the bank could be relieved of restrictions the Federal Reserve had imposed on its activities when we received TARP funding. For example, executive compensation had to be approved by the government-appointed compensation czar, Kenneth R. Feinberg. We also could not engage in certain aspects of new business, such as expanding. The same restrictions were imposed on other firms that received the largest amount of TARP funds.

While the Fed regulated Bank of America Corporation (the holding company) and the OCC regulated Bank of America N.A., or BANA (the bank itself), the FDIC certified the 'soundness' of the bank in terms of its liquidity and safety of operations before it was willing to provide insurance on deposits. As we began to repay our TARP loan, we sought at various intervals to be removed from the jurisdiction of the Fed. At one point, the Fed and the OCC were willing to declare that we had raised enough of the capital mandated by the Stress Test and that our plans going forward were adequate. That would have allowed the restrictions to be lifted. In the end, the FDIC was reluctant to sign off on the soundness of the bank's plans. All of the agencies had to approve our plans.

So, Sheila Bair held all the cards. She certainly lived up to her reputation of being tough on banks, a gutsy FDIC chair who stuck to her guns even when she stood alone in her position. Don Powell arranged for me to meet her to discuss what it would take for her to approve our removal from the TARP restrictions. I would be meeting her for the first time.

On the day of the meeting, Don and I met in Washington, where a limousine service picked us up and drove us to the address we had for the FDIC in Arlington, Virginia. The meeting was at ten o'clock, and we set out well before then. To be late was unthinkable. We arrived at our destination so early that we had a hard time finding someone to let us into the building. We eventually found someone, only to be told that we were at the wrong address.

The wrong address!

How could that be when the words "Federal Deposit Insurance Corporation" were emblazoned out front? It turned out that we were at some sort of satellite office of the FDIC. The chairman's office was located at the agency's headquarters in Washington. We scrambled back into our car and raced back to DC. We barely made it to Chairman Bair's office in time.

As in most of these situations, the head of the agency either makes you wait or is genuinely busy. In this case, we had to wait a few minutes. It actually was quite a pleasant wait because many of the people who worked there — from the receptionist and some of the secretaries to officious-looking individuals walking through the hallways — knew Don when he was chairman from 2001 to 2005, and they stopped to greet him warmly.

Soon we were in Sheila Bair's office. The FDIC chairman was surprisingly short in stature, even shorter than my five-feet-five inches, but she was most formidable in her bearing. We took our seats, Don and I across from each other, Sheila on a couch between us. Sheila had been on the faculty at the University of Massachusetts Amherst at the same time a close friend of mine was provost, so I thought I would ease into the conversation by asking her about UMass Amherst, and if she knew Cora Marrett, the provost. But she was not having any chitchat. This was an official, formal meeting. We weren't old buddies coming in to chat about old friends. Sheila answered my questions politely, but formally. I took the hint.

All the while, I thought she looked at me rather strangely. And I noticed, too, that Don had been trying to get my attention. My chair faced his so I could see his antics. He pointed furtively at my eyeglasses each time Sheila Bair looked away. I finally figured out that I was wearing transition glasses that automatically darken in sunlight and become clear indoors; only mine had not cleared up. They were pitch black. I'm sure I looked like a gangster, a thug at the very least. I finally took off the glasses, and I could see Don breathe a sigh of relief.

In the end, we had a very good conversation with Sheila. She listened carefully to our arguments of why our plan for ending the TARP restrictions should be approved, but she made no promises.

We returned to see her a second time after we began the search process. Our conversation was more relaxed then because we felt we had somewhat gotten to know each other. We had to make sure she was kept abreast of our progress in finding an appropriate successor to Ken.

Luckily, the Search Committee worked well together. We had spirited discussions, and sometimes we disagreed, but we always came together in the end. Like the Special Committee, we met almost twice each week.

I hadn't worked with Chad Holliday or Don Powell before, but they turned out to be perfect colleagues. We even became friends. I've found that when people go through a stressful, intense, critically important process, either they emerge divided — even bitter, and sometimes resentful — or they bond as a team and emerge feeling good about their work. I was fortunate to have colleagues who made good things happen.

As was done with the Special Committee, each member of the Search Committee was assigned to liaise with one or two other members of the board who weren't on the committee. We also maintained ongoing, in-depth contact with constituencies beyond our board, regulators, and supervisors, who also needed to be kept abreast of our progress though not about individual candidates. These constituencies included our major investors — individuals and institutional funds alike. The committee received useful feedback from all of them. Many had specific people to recommend as a successor to Ken, but mostly they talked about the kind of person we ought to be seeking, or about what they saw as the bank's problems and opportunities.

Given all the issues we were dealing with, on the whole, our conversations were far more positive than I expected. Most of those we spoke with believed that the Merrill acquisition would be good in the long run, but felt that the next few years would be challenging for all banks. They advised that our near-term goal should be to raise the capital called for in the Stress Test and to pay off the TARP loans.

A few of these conversations stand out in my mind. One of them was with John Paulson, the hedge fund manager, who foresaw the subprime mortgage crash. He reportedly made four billion dollars when he 'shorted' subprime, mortgage-backed securities in anticipation that their price would fall. Another was with Richard "Dick" Spangler, whose family was the largest single shareholder in Bank of America. His wife, Meredith, was on the board. I had met Dick when he was president of the University of North Carolina, and I was director of the National Science Foundation. We hit it off at that time.

Still another notable conversation was with Tom Marisco, a star mutual fund manager who left Janus Securities to launch his own investment management firm, Marisco Capital. Bank of America bought Marisco Capital in 2000, but Tom bought it back in 2007.

These three men and other individuals with whom I spoke said the bank's long-term prospects were better than what its share price reflected at the time. All of them felt we should raise more capital and pay off the TARP loan as soon as possible. And they all admired Ken in one way or another.

"Ken Lewis will be seen as a patriot when this is all over," one pronounced.

They differed, as did others, on whether or not we should go outside for a new CEO. Some contended that the bank needed someone with a totally different perspective. Others argued strongly against choosing a successor from outside the bank.

"I definitely do not want an outsider. Maybe you can bring back Hugh McColl on an interim basis. I'm sure Hugh would be willing to do it," one of these anti-outsiders suggested.

Then, there were those who took neither side but gave me their full support. As one said, "Walter, you have more power than you think. You can get this done."

I came away from these conversations more encouraged than when I started them. The other members of the Search Committee reported similar, valuable, and encouraging conversations. The feedback we received from the bank's own management and the staff was equally worthwhile. It confirmed our sense that the current management would prefer an insider. However, they were not holding out for an insider at all costs. They were equally concerned we find someone in whom the markets would have confidence, someone who would be seen as the kind of person fit to lead Bank of America.

CHAPTER TWENTY-NINE
STEALTH INTERVIEWS

Steele, Ken, and others told us about the nervousness and uneasiness in the bank over who the new CEO might be. Selecting someone from outside the bank would cause great anxiety. Chief executives at the bank's two key historical components — NationsBank and BankAmerica — had always been company men, at least in recent memory.

The uneasiness grew as our search continued. Our committee was roundly criticized in the press for not moving faster. On October 15th, for example, *Newsweek* wrote, "more than two weeks after announcing his retirement, the bank's board still hasn't named a successor ... The October timing of Lewis's retirement seems to have left Bank of America flat-footed, even though they have had plenty of time to think about it."

These arguments utterly bewildered me.

"How in the world can anyone expect us to name a successor in just two weeks?" I railed to the Search Committee. "They seem to think we have a detailed succession plan in place. We don't! We're going to take the time we need to conduct a thorough, professional, and credible search. After all, Bank of America's new chief will be a key player in the financial world, and our board entrusted us with delivering the best candidate. Those same critics in the press will be the first to condemn us if we settle on anything less."

The search was complicated by the fact that all of the candidates had to consider the enormous challenges the bank faced. Our TARP debt hindered us in executive compensation. We still owed the government forty-five billion dollars; the bank's stock was trading around twelve dollars a share; numerous lawsuits were still hanging, and others were threatened; and Andrew Cuomo, the House Oversight and Government Reform Committee, the SEC, and the Justice Department were still investigating the bank's actions in the acquisition of Merrill.

Cuomo's office did not equivocate. "Ken Lewis's decision to step down will have no impact on our continuing investigation," it announced.

Edolphus Towns, who chaired the House Oversight and Government Reform Committee, was just as quick on the draw. In a statement, he said, "Our investigation has uncovered troubling facts about Bank of America's acquisition of Merrill Lynch, and Mr. Lewis was at the center of this controversy. We hope that Bank of America's new leadership will quickly repay American taxpayers and help us finally resolve unanswered questions."

And yet, we had a fine pool of candidates. Rumors were rife in the press that possible candidates inside the bank were vying for the job. Reuters painted a picture of a 'struggle' involving Sallie Krawcheck, Brian Moynihan, Joe Price, Tom Montag, Greg Curl, and Barbara Desoer, president of the bank's Home Loans division. If this 'struggle' really was taking place, and I don't doubt that it was, it did not reach the level of the board and therefore was not an issue we dealt with.

What we *did* know, and really cared about was the fact that people inside the bank were still working diligently with Ken as a team.

We had already decided to consider both internal and external candidates, and we interviewed the internal people with the same rigor we employed with the external candidates. We still held our meetings at Wachtell, Lipton, Rosen & Katz. In addition to advising the Special Committee, Ed Herlihy was now advising us with the search. Kevin Warsh had warned me to make sure this was not a conflict of interest. With legal counsel, we determined it was not.

We also had contracted Russell Reynolds Associates of Chicago, a professional search firm, which performed the same due diligence on the internal candidates as they did on the external ones. They interviewed third parties about each candidate and looked into any available public information such as their finances and their reputation.

The bank's leadership team seemed pleased with this process. At least, no one complained to me about it. I believe it showed that we were seriously considering one of them to succeed Ken, which, in fact, was true. That was good for morale.

As it also happened, by interviewing internal candidates, we learned a great deal about the internal issues at the bank that normally might not reach the board. This was very helpful in deciding the kind of person we thought we needed as a CEO.

Looking for a CEO is quite different from looking for a board director who essentially serves the institution only part-time. We needed a professional search firm, mainly because many of the possible candidates at this level would likely be a sitting CEO or a top-level executive at another bank. Professional search firms have a reputation for doing their work very delicately. Understandably, very few candidates wanted it to be known that they were being interviewed or were considering leaving their job to go to Bank of America. They were more likely to speak to a search firm because of the very high level of confidentiality such firms offered. Moreover, the top search firms, including Russell Reynolds, knew most of the people we would want to consider. Quite often, these firms had recruited them for the jobs they currently held.

I had worked closely with Russell Reynolds and its co-leader, Charles Tribbett, who lives in Chicago, so we decided to go with them. In cases such as ours, the partner assigned to you is more important than the firm itself. I wanted Charles. He was one of the few African-Americans at the top level of any of the major search firms. He took the case with his team of two.

On their own, the Russell Reynolds team considered nearly one-hundred-and-fifty names and presented fifty or so to the Search Committee. In the end, we interviewed nine individuals in person or by phone before narrowing our choices down to a very small group.

We had to conduct our interviews as though they were stealth operations. All of the candidates held senior positions. Titles varied, but they included chief executives, chief financial officers, chief operating officers, chief risk officers, vice chairman, vice presidents, and divisional presidents. The entire process was exhausting, but it was also instructive. We learned a lot about how our peers and investors viewed the bank, and that knowledge, in turn, influenced our decision-making.

Rumors about potential candidates appeared in the press all the time. Only some of them were accurate. There was also talk that the bank might move its headquarters to New York from Charlotte, and the press took to that with gusto. The likelihood of such a move was of particular concern to the local Charlotte community. The loss of Bank of America as an anchor of the banking industry would be a big blow to the city, which had already lost Wachovia after Wells Fargo acquired it in 2008.

It was true that some of the candidates wanted us to commit to moving the Bank's headquarters to New York. This was not just for their own personal reasons, as is sometimes the case. It's not uncommon for CEOs to want headquarters to be somewhere they want to live. But these candidates' arguments for moving to New York had less to do with personal preference and more to do with being near the office of the New York Federal Reserve, as that would be the bank's primary regulator. The New York Fed has a special place within the banking system. It is generally thought to have a better understanding of the issues major financial firms face. Other than Wells Fargo, all of Bank of America's major competitors were in New York. Some candidates saw our absence as a competitive disadvantage.

Other candidates wanted us to promise to recombine the positions of chairman and CEO. We refused to agree to that.

Given our propensity for leaks, some of the candidates were so gun-shy that we were forced to meet surreptitiously. One candidate, in particular, was much more sensitive than others about being identified. Our committee arranged to meet with him at his home in New York late one Sunday afternoon.

We — Chad Holliday, the two Toms, Don, and I — were staying at the Waldorf Astoria and Towers on Park Avenue in mid-Manhattan. We met in the lobby prior to our appointment with the candidate. It was a dreary, rainy day, and we all wore trench coats, which reinforced the cloak-and-dagger nature of the task at hand.

We were in a good mood, feeling rather smug about the fact that we were going to have this interview, and it wouldn't be leaked to the press.

We stood in a tight circle in the lobby. In addition to the rich, the glamorous, and the famous, the grandeur of the Waldorf Astoria attracted the world's political and business luminaries. The press was never far away.

"Okay, gentlemen. We know this candidate has all the right credentials, excellent track record, and tons of respect in financial and regulatory circles. So, we really want to gauge his interest. Get a feel for what he's like in person," I said to the group, *sotto voce*.

Some nodded. Others muttered their agreement.

"Right. Since we're meeting him where he wanted us to, it should go okay."

More nods. More mutters.

"Let's go, then. But maybe we shouldn't all arrive at his place at the same time."

Just as we were preparing to leave the hotel, Chad Holliday's cell phone rang. Chad stopped, pulled the phone from the inside breast pocket of his jacket, and held it to his ear. Assuming it was a personal call, the rest of us walked ahead a few paces then stopped to wait for him. We were close enough to hear him say, "Chad Holliday," in a brisk, but soft voice.

The silence that followed on his end seemed to stretch out so long that we all turned to stare at him. The phone was still glued to his ear. A deep furrow had appeared on his brow. *Not a good sign,* I thought. *I hope his family is okay.* Then we heard Chad say, "No. Don't do that yet. Hang up. I'll call you right back."

He shoved the phone back into his pocket and moved toward us, swallowing the few feet that separated him from our group in a couple of strides. We watched him uneasily as he approached and closed around him as soon as he reached us. When he spoke, his voice was low and didn't mask his disappointment.

"He says he's sorry to have to do it, but he has to cancel our meeting. He says the press found out about it somehow, and he thinks they're staking out his home."

Jaws dropped.

"Here we go again!"

"How in the world do they find out these things?"

"Is he sure?"

"Who, besides us, knew about this meeting?"

I didn't think it was Dan Fitzpatrick who had initiated the leak. I believed it probably was someone in his organization. Vexing as this was, we could not let it stop us from having our meeting.

"Let's not worry now about who leaked it or how it was done. We need to keep this meeting on," I said. "Any ideas?"

"Let him meet us here."

I can't remember who said that, but we soon came up with what we felt was a sound plan. Since he lived nearby, the candidate could come to the Waldorf instead. He should set out ostensibly for a leisurely walk and slip into the hotel. We would meet him there.

Chad relayed our plan to the candidate, and he agreed to it. We had no idea if it would work. The candidate might decide to stay home instead. An enterprising reporter might follow him into the hotel. Anything could foil the plan.

Miraculously, it worked. We had a good meeting. The candidate expressed serious interest.

Our good feelings didn't last. Much to our frustration, the candidate's job at the time made his situation so sensitive that we had to reschedule, move to different venues, or altogether cancel subsequent meetings at his behest.

In retrospect, the Committee's predicament with this particular candidate was almost comic. It just didn't seem funny at the time. We began to ask ourselves if the candidate really wanted the job. Was his interest solid enough to see his candidacy through to the end both sides hoped for? If it was, what might his terms be?

The answers would come later.

CHAPTER THIRTY
A SUCCESSOR AT LAST

I was becoming extremely agitated, not just because of the elusive candidate, but also because of our general lack of progress. We were not moving as fast as I had hoped. Kevin Warsh's admonition, "You can't waste any time on this, Walter," kept replaying in my mind.

I was having more trouble sleeping than usual and found myself easily irritated over relatively small things, like missing shots on the tennis court, or meetings not starting on time. I tried to hide my exasperation from my colleagues on the Search Committee because I didn't want them to lose confidence in me.

Fortunately, I could show my true feelings to Shirley. She was great. She insisted that we try to do more of the things we liked — dining out, listening to jazz, going to the symphony, and dancing, even at home in the kitchen.

It was also a blessing to have Alice working so closely with me. I confided almost everything in her, though never the names of candidates. I could show my frustration, irritation, and even anger, in her presence, and she would quickly placate me.

"Calm down, Walter. Watch your blood pressure," she would say, or something to that effect.

We were nearing mid-November. Ken would be retiring in six weeks, and we still weren't making appreciable headway in finding a successor. The situation threatened to disrupt important plans Shirley and I had made earlier.

Back in August, we hadn't yet known about Ken's plans; we seemed to be making substantial progress in our agreement with the Fed, and so Shirley and I booked an Atlantic crossing. We planned our trip for November. We were going to take the Queen Mary 2 from England to New York, and we were both looking forward to taking a break from the stress and pace of my chairmanship. The trip was also meant to be a belated celebration of our 40th wedding anniversary.

Two days before we were scheduled to depart — by which time Shirley had finished packing, and our tickets were in hand — we had yet another scheduled meeting with our slippery candidate. This time it was at New York's Battery Park Ritz Carlton. We had reserved a conference room and were waiting for our candidate to arrive when the phone rang.

"I'm afraid I have to disappoint you again. The word is out in my company that I'm seeing you guys. I can't meet with you."

He didn't sound contrite at all.

The whole team was taken aback. All the pressure of the search — the subterfuge, postponements, the back-and-forth travel — reached a boiling point.

I exploded. "This is unbelievable!"

I stormed out of the conference room, visibly overwrought. My reaction alarmed my colleagues. I rarely behaved that way around them. Usually, I was the one who tried to keep everyone calm.

I phoned Shirley as soon as I was outside the conference room.

"Shirley, unpack, and cancel the trip!"

I didn't realize how loud my voice was or how upset I sounded.

"What's the matter?" Shirley demanded.

Shirley is the proverbial 'trooper.' She's very flexible. She worries about things, but she doesn't spend an inordinate amount of time worrying. She has an attitude that cuts to the chase, one that says, "Okay, let's just carry on."

Several years ago, for example, we were visiting our son in Amsterdam, and she fell and hit her head on the sidewalk as we walked to dinner. She was always tripping. People in the apartments above heard us shouting. Some kids ran downstairs with ice. Shirley had a colossal knot on her head.

"Shirley, we need to go to the hospital. We should go to the hospital," our son and I kept insisting.

"No!"

She tightened her lips, which signaled the futility of further argument on that score.

"Then let's go back to the hotel," I said.

"No! We have to go to dinner."

She wouldn't budge, so we continued on our way. Incredibly, Shirley sat through dinner, holding an icepack on the bump on her head. She ate, drank, and had a great time. Our waitress didn't know what to make of this, but she took it upon herself to bring fresh ice several times throughout the meal. Diners nearby stared at us, baffled by the whole scene. They must have been thinking, "There go those crazy Americans again."

On another occasion, we were walking toward Millennium Park in Chicago, on our way to dinner with friends, and Shirley fell — again. This time she broke a tooth. True to character, she insisted on going to dinner with our friends, which we did. She went to the dentist the next day and had to have her broken tooth replaced.

She was no different when I said she should unpack and cancel our Queen Mary 2 trip. Her attitude was, "Well, what do I have to do? I don't know if we'll get our money back for the tickets because I'm not sure we've got insurance. All right. I have to do this, and this, and this." She muttered some of this aloud.

I was sure that even before I finished explaining what was happening, she had already drawn up in her head a list of what she needed to do to cancel the trip. Our plans had been changing so much lately — I would have to attend a meeting suddenly, cancel dinners, and so on — that she was getting used to making alternative arrangements at the last minute.

Still, I'm positive she was very disappointed in this instance because we were supposed to be celebrating our wedding anniversary. We had been planning the trip for nearly a year, and we're really looking forward to the black-tie dinners and dancing to a big band, as the ship's brochures advertised.

"We are just not making progress on this search, and I can't leave!" I explained to Shirley now. My voice was still raised.

I didn't have a chance to hear her response. Chad Gifford and Don Powell came running from the conference room. They had overheard me.

"What are you doing, Walter? Don't cancel your trip. Don't do that!" Chad shouted.

"I'll call you back," I said to Shirley and hung up.

Don's eyes bored into mine. I still hear the authority in his voice, with that Texas drawl, when I recall that moment.

"Walter, you go on that ship with your wife. What's going on in that conference room isn't life. Your being on that ship with your wife is life. We can handle things here."

By that time, the whole committee was urging me to go.

"We'll keep working, Walter."

"Yes. And we'll arrange a call to the ship every day so we can fill you in and get your feedback."

I was still reluctant to go on the trip, given our circumstances. We had already been criticized in the press for taking so long with the search. Time was running out. People in the bank were beginning to be concerned that we weren't finding anyone. So how would it look for the chairman of the Search Committee, the chairman of the board, to be on a ship in the middle of the Atlantic when we were supposed to be conducting one of the most important searches in the world of finance? I was really worried about that.

In the end, my team convinced me that I should go on the trip.

"Don't worry, Walter. We'll figure out a way to make it look like you're right here with us," Don said.

"That's easy. One of us will call you every day." It was either one of the Chads or one of the Toms who said that.

I was moved and immensely grateful.

Only the committee members were supposed to know that I was not in New York or Charlotte but on the Queen Mary 2. I had admonished Alice, and Susan, my secretary at the bank in Chicago, not to say where I was if I got calls or emails.

I still had a part-time secretary at Morehouse as part of my retirement benefits as president, and I'd kept her even after I became chairman of the bank. But no one, not even I, remembered to tell Bobbie. Although I had kept her on, I rarely needed her services now that I had a full-time secretary at Bank of America.

Somehow, *USA Today* located her. When they called her, she innocently said, "Oh, he's on a cruise and can't be reached now."

Bobbie contacted me on the ship and told me about her conversation with *USA Today*.

"What! This is it," I thought dismally. "The press is going to have a grand time."

USA Today ran with the story. Amazingly, the article appeared only in that paper. It was a small article, and nobody else picked it up — not even Dan Fitzpatrick. It was mind-boggling.

The committee worked hard during my absence and telephoned me as promised. Tom, Chad, or some other member of the committee called me every day, or we would have a conference call with the full committee.

As the ship traveled from Southampton to New York, we gained an hour every night. The time change relative to New York meant I was on the phone at different times each day. This was cause for some pretty hilarious moments on board the ship. I had to leave Shirley alone at public get-togethers every night and disappear for a long phone meeting with the committee. Fellow travelers would see us at dinner together, and then they would see me leave for an hour or so but not always at the same time each night. I am sure some of them wondered about the kind of marriage we had, and whether we were really celebrating our anniversary.

Shirley remained her usual self. She concocted excuses, chatted away, and engaged in small talk.

Once we arrived in New York, I went to WRLK. I had been given the use of an office there and planned to work alone before calling a meeting of the committee. We all felt that we just had to bring the search to a close.

By then, we had settled on a small number of candidates we wanted to interview again to make a final list. Among them was Brian Moynihan. In many ways, he was my benchmark. I had always thought that anyone we hired from the outside had to be at least as good as Brian, preferably even better. Bringing in an external candidate who did not live up to that standard certainly would not go over well inside the bank. And based on the conversations we had had with major investors, it would not have been received well in the marketplace either.

From the very beginning of the search, several people had speculated that Brian was a leading candidate. There were rumors, too, that Chad Gifford and Tom May favored him, and were pushing for him because he had worked with them at Fleet. Rumors were all they were. Although Chad and Tom never hid their admiration and respect for Brian, neither indicated any predisposed bias toward him during the search.

Brian had been the bank's General Counsel for a brief period during the Merrill transaction and had received some negative press over his testimony on the deal to the House Committee on Oversight and Government Reform on November 17th. Bloomberg News quoted Committee Chair, Edolphus Towns, as saying in its interview with him, "I didn't find some of his answers believable. He didn't show the kind of leadership a company would seem to need."

And, after hearing Brian's testimony, Bloomberg reported in the same article that Committee member Elijah Cummings had said to him, "I don't know who you think we are, but I find some of the things you said not believable."

But Brian had also occupied several important positions at Fleet, and subsequently at Bank of America, and knew the bank very well, including its challenges and opportunities. The feedback from our queries and from Russell Reynolds was consistent: Brian was very smart. He was hardworking and respected, but it was his intellect; we knew we couldn't pass him up.

After the Search Committee interviewed him for a second time, we unanimously decided to recommend him to the full board. We now had to inform the Fed, but we decided to hold off until just before the board meeting as an indication that we were not asking for permission, but simply informing them.

On the afternoon of Wednesday, December 16th, two hours before the board meeting, the full Search Committee gathered in a small conference room at the bank's headquarters in Charlotte. We had arranged a call with Kevin Warsh. We had no idea what his or Ben Bernanke's reaction would be, but we were prepared to push back if it was negative. After all, Kevin had stipulated that the decision of who would become the new CEO rested with the board, not the Fed. All they wanted was our assurance that we would carry out a "thorough, professional, and credible" search, which we had done.

Nevertheless, we all were visibly nervous when I dialed Kevin's number. I greeted Kevin as soon as he picked up.

"Hello, Kevin. Walter here. How are you doing?"

"Doing okay. I hear you have news for us."

"Yes, we have finished the search, and in about two hours, we are going to be recommending to the full board that Brian Moynihan succeed Ken as our next CEO."

I had turned on the speakerphone so the entire committee could hear both sides of the conversation. They anxiously leaned in.

I continued. "Kevin, I can assure you that we did a very open and thorough search, and Brian emerged as our unanimous choice. I have the other committee members here if you have questions."

We practically held our breath in the pause before Kevin spoke.

Then, in that same calm, measured voice as always, he said, "Walter, this is an excellent choice. Ben will be pleased."

Whoa! We silently high-fived each other across the table.

"All of you did a great job. Congratulations!" Kevin said.

We looked at each other, grinning with relief. After we hung up, we talked about how we did not expect such a quick positive reaction. We were feeling good. One hurdle crossed. Now on to the full board.

It was never up to the Search Committee to decide who would be the CEO. We were pretty confident that the board would accept our recommendation, but we couldn't, on our own, make this decision. And, as slight as it might be, there was always a chance that the board might not go along with our choice.

It was still a relatively new board. Some of the directors had worked with Brian for years. Others had worked with him at Fleet. And there were those who had only recently joined the board and didn't know him well at all, so we couldn't presume that the full board would automatically accept our decision. We had to present strong arguments to show the board why we thought Brian was the best candidate. Charles Tribbett and Clarke Murphy, Charles's associate from Russell Reynolds, would also attend the meeting so the board could ask them questions about the process we had gone through, and the other candidates we had interviewed.

It was critical that all this be explained because there were those, including some of the candidates, who felt that the choice of the CEO was fixed for an internal candidate. Brian or someone else inside the bank was going to get the job anyway, they believed. The committee and the search firm, therefore, had to convey the seriousness of the search, and the fact that Brian rose to the top as a result of a thorough, comprehensive, and detailed process.

Evidently, we did our job; the board voted unanimously to accept our recommendation.

Brian had been an obvious candidate from the time Ken announced his decision to leave. His selection was popular inside the bank and was greeted positively in the press.

"Brian Moynihan is a team player," *Institutional Investor* declared. "Bank of America needs Moynihan more than ever now."

Analysts also had plenty to say.

"Moynihan was our top pick," one told *Institutional Investor*. "If you think they have a working business model, he would be the perfect guy. An internal candidate was clearly the best path. It's great news for BofA."

The Associated Press interviewed several others and reported their comments.

"My concern about bringing in an external candidate was that somebody would come in and feel the need to put their stamp on the company through a restructuring or through a period of turbulence. The bank just doesn't need that right now. An internal candidate who knows the players and who knows what needs to be done ... is probably a wise choice at this point."

By picking someone from within, another said, "you express an ability to create a culture that can produce leaders, and that's very important."

News organizations also reported on speculation that Brian had been Ken's choice all along. He may have been, but Ken never pushed the committee in any direction. I knew he hoped we would choose someone from the inside, so he got his wish.

Blessedly, after eleven weeks of what a University of North Carolina at Charlotte professor aptly termed "probably the executive search from hell," there would be someone to take the reins from Ken on December 31st.

For me, there was another bit of pleasure in this choice: Brian had been a student at Brown when I was Dean of the College. Although I didn't know him then, he knew me. It was great to see one of 'my students' reach the top.

We had our successor at last. Maybe now I could be a 'normal' non-executive Chairman.

CHAPTER THIRTY-ONE

FINALLY THE 'NORMAL'
I HAD ENVISIONED

The final months of that exasperating, but an utterly fulfilling year of my life seemed to go by rather quickly after the Search Committee had done its job.

We had to integrate the Merrill Lynch operation and deal with increasing losses from the Countrywide acquisition. But we no longer needed the Special Committee, nor, of course, the Search Committee.

From January 1, 2010, when Brian assumed the CEO position until I retired as chairman in April, my chairmanship was more like the 'normal' role I had first envisioned: keeping a steady hand on the tiller, making sure the board worked.

Brian and I worked very well together, just as Ken and I had, although Brian was a new CEO adjusting to being in charge. As one pundit said, "The only preparation for being a CEO is being a CEO." I don't recall where I heard that statement before, but I certainly found it to be valid in my first CEO role as director of Argonne National Laboratory.

I had been commuting every week to Charlotte from Chicago, but now, more like a normal chairman, I made the trip only once every two weeks or so. And I had an office in Chicago, in the beautiful, historic building that housed the LaSalle Bank, which was renamed Bank of America after we had purchased it in 2007.

Given all that the bank and my team and I had endured, and even with the challenges that remained, I felt the period from January 1, 2010, were the halcyon days of my chairmanship.

I presided over my last Bank of America board meeting on April 27, 2010, the eve of that year's annual shareholders meeting.

The night before, the board hosted a special dinner to which Shirley was invited. That was the first time she met most of the people I'd been talking about for a year. The only person she knew was Chad Gifford, from our visit to Nantucket.

It was a fun occasion. Shirley and I talked about all the working evenings and weekends that left her and other spouses alone, and about what it was like for her on the Queen Mary 2 when she had to explain my disappearances. Don Powell was in his very best charming, Texas gentleman persona. He and Shirley really hit it off. She told him how happy she was that he insisted I take the Queen Mary 2 cruise in spite of all the work to be done.

The next night, Brian and his senior managers hosted a small, informal dinner for us. It was touching to hear Brian thank not just me but also Shirley for her contribution to the bank's success, and receiving the wonderful parting gift that he and his team had paid for out of their own pockets — a one-week trip, first-class, to anywhere in the world we chose.

I came away from those events immensely pleased with what we had all accomplished during that frantic year. We had chosen a new chief executive; reconstituted the board of directors; reorganized the board's committees; repaid the government's $45 billion, with interest; removed the uncertainty about the bank's solvency and operating performance, and modified our operations to fit a new world. Our shareholder constituents earned a 105 percent return from the day I took over to the day I retired, as the bank's stock went from $8.80 a share to about $18.

The Merrill deal turned out to be most worthwhile. The synergies we envisioned did materialize. The investment bank and wealth management divisions have been among the most profitable divisions of the bank in recent years. On the other hand, the Countrywide acquisition, which was not controversial at all at the time, has proven to be a disaster, with total losses of over $50 billion. And we racked up more billions in lawsuits and federal fines. Yet, the bank is prospering under Brian's leadership as I write this memoir, totally validating our selection of him as CEO.

Yes. I felt very good about my chairmanship. Evidently, so did others. The board gave me the lifetime title of "Retired Chairman of Bank of America." A board member emailed me the following note after reading sections of this memoir before it was published.

"Walter – and I mean this – you should take pride in what was accomplished: 1) BAC survived, and that wasn't a given, and 2) electing Brian (also not a given) who is increasingly seen as one of the very best banking CEOs. All this while constantly dealing with very nervous regulators."

One of the most enjoyable and gratifying aspects of this entire adventure was working closely, very closely, with colleagues like the two Chads, the two Toms, Frank, Don, Charles, and all of my other team members. I do think of us as a team. I now understand the sentiments athletes express after they have won a big game or tournament. That thrilling sense of camaraderie, that pride of collective achievement experienced all too infrequently in life.

I also learned a lot. Not just about the functioning of our nation's financial system, its strengths, and vulnerabilities, but also about my own capabilities. When we were working nonstop in the eye of the storm, there was no time to really reflect on the significance of our undertaking. It was only afterward that I realized how much I was in the spotlight, not just for the regulators, shareholders, and media, but also for the three-hundred-thousand or so Bank of America employees and associates.

On my last flight on a bank plane, after we landed, the pilot approached me as I exited. "Dr. Massey, thank you for all you did to save the bank," he said.

Quite often after that, I would encounter bank employees — officers, tellers, secretaries — who thanked me for 'saving our jobs.'

It's probably a good thing that I did not have time to think about how many people — real people, not abstract entities — depended on our doing our job right.

Of the many complimentary notes I received after I stepped down, I am most proud of one from a non-board member colleague who wrote, "Walter, I am glad we got the chance to work together during your tenure as chairman at Bank of America. You exerted a tremendous steadying, calming, and healing influence. You were steady and determined: you listened a lot to your colleagues and advisors, but in the end, you made sure things got done, and decisions got made. The response to the (Fed mandate) was as seamless as I have ever seen to such a significant enforcement action, and without your management of the process and your efforts to cultivate good relations with the regulators that simply couldn't have happened. You guided a CEO search under highly pressured circumstances and, as we now see, delivered a great result. I hope you derive great satisfaction from the fact that through your personal efforts and commitment you've set BofA on a healthy, stable course for the future."

To the extent that those words are reflective of a larger audience, I am very proud to have been part of this experience. My time as chairman at Bank of America was a period highlighting a crisis in leadership. It taught me a great deal about leadership, about working with others, and how business, politics, and government are interconnected.

I had leapt into the eye of a storm and emerged more learned, with no regrets.

I have continued to be eager to try new challenges that push me into uncharted territory. My two recent activities as president and chancellor of the School of the Art Institute of Chicago (SAIC) and chairman of the board of the Giant Magellan Telescope Organization (GMTO) are examples of what I said at the beginning — that my life is like the lines of an abstract painting. The next project is a stroke that won't be an easy straight line.

I am ready now to proceed with my next memoirs, driven by the new perspectives I have gained about leadership, on the one hand, and on the other by the need for the worlds of business, art, science, and technology to work together for the betterment of society.

I accept the fact that my world will always be one where the theme changes and, like the amazing mosaic of a nonrepresentational work of art, makes sense in the end. This is my life's 'normal.'

I hope that I have encouraged every reader to be dauntless and courageous when considering a new barrier-breaking path in life.

Take the leap. What can you lose?

INDEX

231